FOUR SEASO SALADS

FOUR SEASONS
SALADS

Jackie Burrow

CONTENTS

ANOTHER BEST-SELLING VOLUME FROM HPBooks®

Publisher: Rick Bailey; Editorial Director: Elaine R. Woodard
Editor: Jeanette P. Egan; Art Director: Don Burton
Book Assembly: Leslie Sinclair
Typography: Cindy Coatsworth, Michelle Claridge
Book Manufacture: Anthony B. Narducci
Recipe testing by International Cookbook Services: Barbara Bloch,
President; Rita Barrett, Director of Testing

Published by HPBooks, Inc.
P.O. Box 5367, Tucson, AZ 85703 602/888-2150
ISBN 0-89586-344-8
Library of Congress Catalog Card Number 85-60084
© 1985 HPBooks, Inc. Printed in the U.S.A.
1st Printing

Originally published as Four Seasons Salads
© 1983 Hennerwood Publications Limited

Cover Photo: Medley of salads and ingredients for the four seasons

Introduction

Gone are the days when salads were only served on hot summer days and always consisted of lettuce, tomato and cucumber. Now salads are served all year around and include numerous exciting ingredients. Salads are served for all occasions and range from substantial main courses to colorful side dishes and sophisticated starters. They may be simple to prepare, requiring only a few minutes to assemble before serving, or they may involve more elaborate preparations that can be done ahead.

Whichever type of salad you choose, it will always be fun to put together. Interesting salads consist of contrasting flavors, colors and textures. Preparing a salad is a wonderful excuse to indulge your imagination in arranging ingredients and in trying new garnishes. The presentation of a salad is all-important. Look for interesting plates and dishes for serving. Wooden salad bowls are perfect for green salads, but do not show off more elaborate salads to advantage. Use attractive glass, china or pottery serving plates, bowls and platters for these. It's fun to serve ethnic dishes in their native pottery. Many salads look their prettiest when arranged in individual dishes.

The recipes in this book are arranged according to the four seasons of the year. In each season you will find a selection of recipes for starters, main dishes and dinner salads. Starters are designed to stimulate the appetite; therefore, serving size should be smaller than those for most dinner salads and main dishes. Several light main-dishes are included; these are perfect for suppers and lunches. Dinner salads can vary from a simple tossed salad to a hearty bean or potato salad. The inspiration for these recipes comes from all over the world. This wide range of cuisines adds variety in flavor and texture, and introduces lots of new ideas for combining and presenting familiar and exotic ingredients.

Since most ingredients are fresh and seasonal, all the salads are healthy and nutritious. Some salads are ideal for those watching calories. But beware of calorie-laden ingredients, such as cheese, nuts, avocados and some dressings. Because salads are served chilled or at room temperature, they are excellent choices for make-ahead entertaining, as well as for family meals.

SALAD DRESSINGS

The dressing is a vitally important element of any salad. It can literally make or break a salad's success. There are numerous types of dressing; choose one according to the ingredients you have available and the salad it is destined to dress. The classic vinaigrette or oil-and-vinegar dressing must be made with the best quality oil and vinegar. The exact proportions will depend on the types of oil and vinegar used and personal preference. This dressing should always be made to taste. A good oil-and-vinegar dressing is indispensable if you make salads regularly. Make and store it in a screw-top jar. Remember to shake the jar vigorously to combine the dressing before using. Oil-and-vinegar dressings can be refrigerated up to one week. Mayonnaise is another classic dressing that can be served with most salads. Homemade mayonnaise is not difficult to make and is more flavorful than commercially prepared ones.

Many other ingredients may be used in salad dressings. Yogurt, sour cream, cheeses, honey, sugar, garlic, herbs, citrus juices and other fruit juices are just a few. It's fun to experiment with different combinations.

Delicate fresh salad greens should be dressed immediately before serving; dressings cause them to wilt. The more robust greens and root vegetables can be dressed ahead. This will allow the vegetables to soften and flavors to blend. Starchy salad ingredients, such as potatoes, rice, pasta and dry beans, improve in flavor if dressed while still hot. This allows them to absorb more flavor from the dressing.

Recipes for mayonnaise and other salad dressings can be found on pages 78 and 79.

SPRING

Spring is the season when the days grow warmer and light meals have more appeal. This is also a good time to lose any extra pounds that might have crept on during the winter months. Spring, however, is often the most difficult time of year to find salad ingredients, either in the markets or in the vegetable garden. The home-grown, common salad vegetables, such as lettuce, cucumbers and tomatoes, are not yet ready for eating. Only the more expensive greenhouse and imported varieties can be found.

Fortunately, there are other vegetables available at this time with which to make delicious salads—for example, artichokes and asparagus. These are at their best in the spring. These two vegetables make luxurious salads. Cook simply and serve chilled with mayonnaise or oil-and-vinegar dressing. Or, combine these with other ingredients to make a more economical salad. In early spring, when there are few salad greens around, make use of root vegetables and green-leafy vegetables, such as carrots, potatoes and cabbage. Served in interesting dressings, these make excellent salads, either raw or cooked.

Dried legumes are another useful standby when fresh vegetables are scarce and expensive. Black-eyed peas, lima beans, kidney beans and lentils all make delicious economical starters and dinner salads. Cook and combine with contrasting ingredients and a good salad dressing. Bean sprouts and alfalfa sprouts are other valuable additions to salads when other vegetables are scarce. Small young spinach leaves can be used raw or lightly cooked to make nutritious salads. Other versatile ingredients include avocados, citrus fruits and pineapples. Later in the spring, delicious new potatoes and sweet young carrots increase the repertoire of salad vegetables.

SUMMER

Summer is the time for eating outdoors, picnics and barbecues. As summer approaches, all fresh salad ingredients become more economical and more plentiful. Early summer is a good time to make salads from leaf lettuce and some of the spring vegetables that are still available.

Tomatoes, cucumbers, sweet peppers, zucchini, eggplant and other vegetables are featured in the markets and in vegetable gardens. These are all delicious additions to salads. Except for eggplant, most of these vegetables can be served either raw or cooked. Cook eggplant before using. Tomatoes are invaluable for evoking a wonderful Mediterranean-feel in salads. Summer is also the time for fresh green beans and peas. Fresh young lima beans, sugar peas and Chinese pea pods are excellent raw in salads. Cook green beans and more mature pea pods until crisp-tender before using. Beets and corn are ready for picking; when cooked, they make colorful additions to salads.

Fresh herbs are available throughout the summer. They add color and flavor to salads. Some, such as parsley, fennel and chives, can be chopped finely and included as an ingredient or as a garnish. Others, such as basil, sage, dill and marjoram, can be added to dressings in small quantities to add flavor. Many fresh herbs are relatively easy to grow yourself, either in the garden or in window boxes. These include mint, basil, thyme, chives, marjoram, tarragon and parsley.

For luxurious main-dish salads, use salmon or other fish and seafood. Summer fruits, such as strawberries, raspberries, peaches and melons, can be added to other ingredients or used on their own. Fill small melon halves or quarters with a fruit salad or a seafood mixture for an attractive presentation.

AUTUMN

Orchard fruits, such as apples and pears, herald the beginning of autumn. Grapes are also plentiful in early autumn. Combine these fruits with savory foods for salads. Or, use a combination of fruits to make a tasty fruit salad. Some summer vegetables, such as tomatoes, zucchini, eggplant, bell peppers and green beans, are also still in good supply in early autumn. When summer vegetables start to disappear, take advantage of those ingredients that are available in the markets all year long. One example of these is cultivated mushrooms. Look for new varieties, such as enoki mushrooms, that are becoming more widely available.

Celery, Chinese cabbage and fennel are plentiful now. Use these as interesting raw additions to autumn salads. Leeks are also beginning to reappear in the markets. A relatively new vegetable to look for is jícama. Its crisp texture adds a nice crunchiness to salads.

With the onset of winter, fresh salad greens and fresh herbs are more expensive. Rely instead on capers, pickles, anchovies and olives for flavoring and garnishing. Use nuts and dried fruits to liven up salads. *Fennel & Apple Salad*, page 48, combines two autumn favorites—fennel and apples.

Selection of salad ingredients

WINTER

Winter sees the return of favorite vegetables which have been absent during the summer months. These include leeks; red, green and white cabbage; broccoli; cauliflower; and Brussels sprouts. Many of these vegetables are best after a frost. They can be finely shredded and eaten raw or lightly cooked. Root vegetables, such as carrots, celeriac, turnips and kohlrabies, are also good salad ingredients. Grate or finely chop these for eating raw, or cook these until crisp-tender. Chicory and cabbage are great winter-salad standbys and can be used instead of lettuce. They both keep well in the refrigerator. Radicchio, a very attractive, small red chicory, is an unusual and delicious addition to winter salads. It is not widely available and may be expensive, but a little adds color and flavor.

Sunchokes, also called Jerusalem artichokes, tend to be an underrated vegetable. They are also a delicious addition to salads. Around Christmas, there is an excellent supply of fresh nuts. These include chestnuts, pecans, almonds, Brazil nuts and walnuts. They are excellent in salads, especially when combined with dried fruits. Citrus fruits are in season. The tartness and flavor of oranges, tangerines and grapefruit make good contrasts to less assertive salad ingredients. Or, try other fruits, such as pomegranates and cranberries, to add color and flavor. For main-dish salads and starters, use the shellfish and fish that are available.

Ingredients for autumn and winter salads

VEGETABLE CALENDAR

PEAK SEASON IS SHOWN IN GRAY.

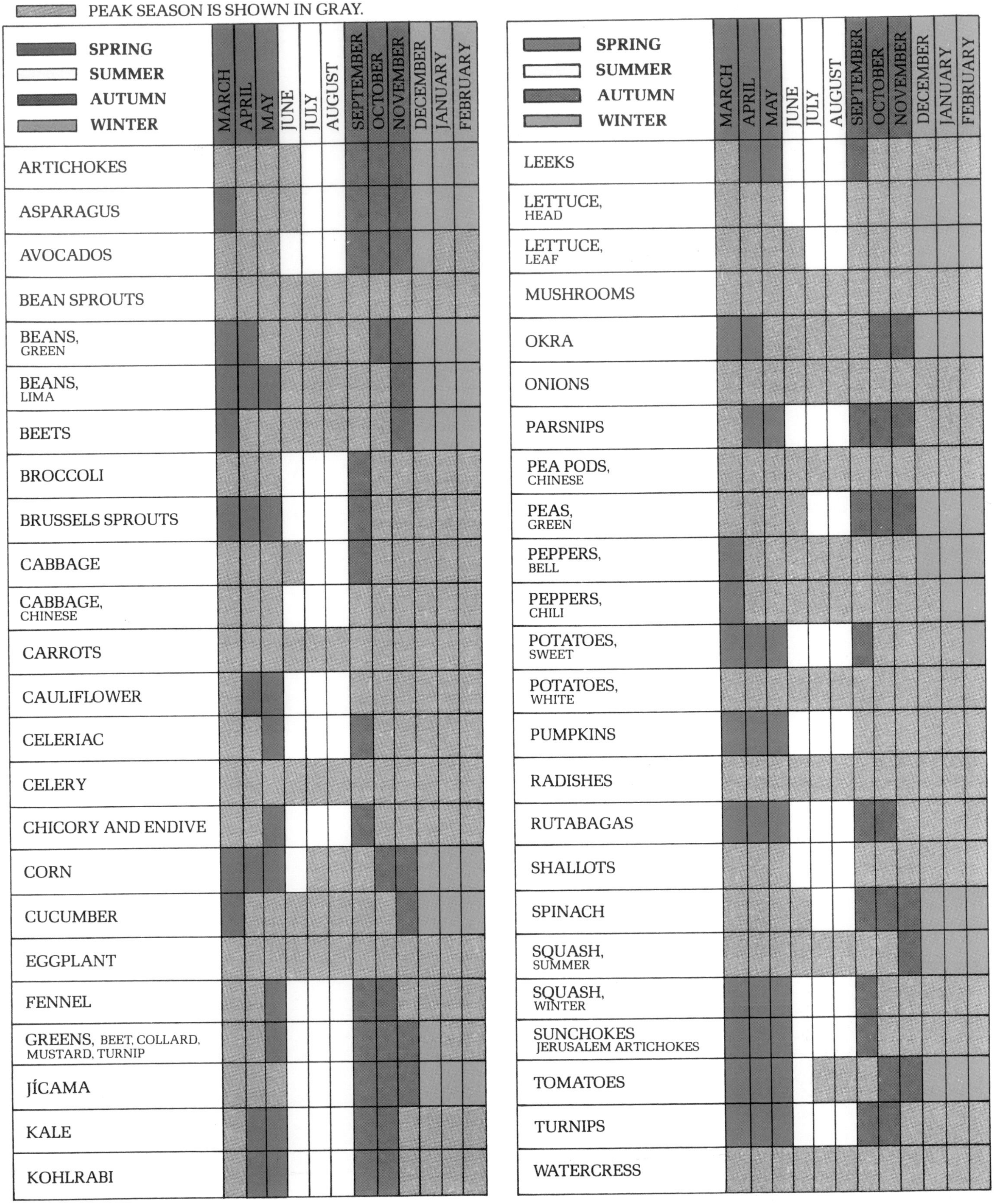

Legend: SPRING · SUMMER · AUTUMN · WINTER

Months (columns): MARCH, APRIL, MAY, JUNE, JULY, AUGUST, SEPTEMBER, OCTOBER, NOVEMBER, DECEMBER, JANUARY, FEBRUARY

Left column vegetables:

- ARTICHOKES
- ASPARAGUS
- AVOCADOS
- BEAN SPROUTS
- BEANS, GREEN
- BEANS, LIMA
- BEETS
- BROCCOLI
- BRUSSELS SPROUTS
- CABBAGE
- CABBAGE, CHINESE
- CARROTS
- CAULIFLOWER
- CELERIAC
- CELERY
- CHICORY AND ENDIVE
- CORN
- CUCUMBER
- EGGPLANT
- FENNEL
- GREENS, BEET, COLLARD, MUSTARD, TURNIP
- JÍCAMA
- KALE
- KOHLRABI

Right column vegetables:

- LEEKS
- LETTUCE, HEAD
- LETTUCE, LEAF
- MUSHROOMS
- OKRA
- ONIONS
- PARSNIPS
- PEA PODS, CHINESE
- PEAS, GREEN
- PEPPERS, BELL
- PEPPERS, CHILI
- POTATOES, SWEET
- POTATOES, WHITE
- PUMPKINS
- RADISHES
- RUTABAGAS
- SHALLOTS
- SPINACH
- SQUASH, SUMMER
- SQUASH, WINTER
- SUNCHOKES, JERUSALEM ARTICHOKES
- TOMATOES
- TURNIPS
- WATERCRESS

UNUSUAL VEGETABLES

The following vegetables are unusual in one or two ways. Either they are not as familiar and widely available as the usual tomato, radish or cucumber, or they are not normally thought of as ingredients for salads—for example, lima beans and cauliflower.

ARTICHOKE

Member of the thistle family. The fat bases of the leaves are edible, and artichoke bottoms and hearts are considered delicacies.

Preparation—Cut off stalks to make a level base. Pull off any tough outer leaves; cut off tips of remaining leaves. Cook in boiling salted water 30 to 40 minutes or until a leaf pulls out easily. Drain upside-down until cold. Remove choke, page 26.

Serving ideas—Serve as a starter with oil-and-vinegar dressing, mayonnaise or hollandaise sauce for dipping. Or, remove and discard chokes from cooked artichokes; stuff with a salad mixture. Serve hearts on their own or with other ingredients for hors d'oeuvres. Artichoke hearts are available frozen and canned.

ASPARAGUS

Stalks 6 to 8 inches long. Asparagus can be green or white, thin or thick. Tips and most of stalk are edible.

Preparation—Wash; break off woody ends. Tie in bundles. Cook upright, so the stalks cook in the boiling water while the tips cook in the steam above. Stalks take longer to cook than tips. Cook in boiling salted water about 15 minutes or until crisp-tender. When cooking white asparagus, add a little lemon juice to the water to keep the asparagus white.

Serving ideas—Cooked asparagus can be eaten hot or cold. Serve as a starter with oil-and-vinegar dressing, mayonnaise or hollandaise sauce. Asparagus is also available canned and frozen.

AVOCADO

A pear-shaped tropical fruit with a dark-green skin.

Preparation—Use raw for salads. Cut in half with a stainless-steel knife; remove seed. If only 1/2 of avocado will be used, do not remove seed. Rub cut surfaces with lemon juice immediately to prevent browning.

Serving ideas—Serve unpeeled halves filled with oil-and-vinegar dressing. Or, stuff with a seafood salad. Cube or slice peeled avocados for salads. This adds an interesting flavor and texture. Puree to make guacamole.

BEANS, BROAD

Large beans with a whitish skin and bright-green flesh. They are usually sold in their pods.

Preparation—Remove from pods; peel more mature beans. Cook in boiling salted water 25 to 30 minutes, depending on age, or until tender. Drain and cool.

Serving ideas—Serve in an oil-and-vinegar dressing or a yogurt dressing with herbs. Serve as a dinner salad or as part of an hors d'oeuvre.

BEANS, GREEN

Best in summer.

Preparation—Young tender green beans can be trimmed and left whole. Remove strings from more mature beans; slice diagonally. Boil in salted water about 10 minutes or until crisp-tender. Drain and cool. Canned and frozen green beans can also be used for salads.

Serving ideas—Serve alone in a dressing, or as part of an arranged salad, such as a salad Niçoise.

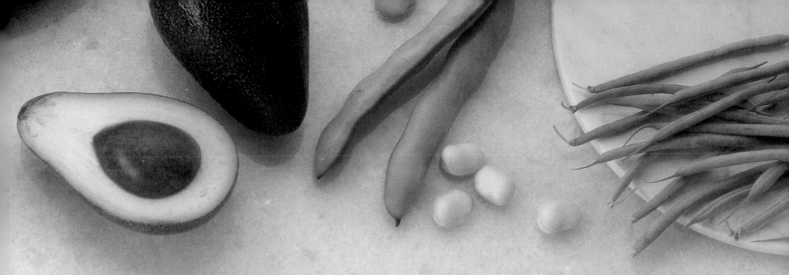

BEAN SPROUTS

Sprouts from dried beans, usually mung or soy, page 23.

Preparation—Wash well; drain. Serve raw. Canned bean sprouts are not suitable for salads.

Serving ideas—Serve with oriental ingredients. Or, add to a tossed green salad to give extra crunchiness.

BROCCOLI

Available year around; best during the cooler months. Buds should be tightly closed.

Preparation—Cut into small pieces; serve raw. Or, divide into flowerets; boil in salted water 5 to 8 minutes, depending on thickness of stalks, or until crisp-tender. Drain and cool.

Serving ideas—Serve as a starter with hollandaise sauce, or combine with other ingredients in a mixed salad.

BRUSSELS SPROUTS

Member of the cabbage family. Best during cooler months.

Preparation—Finely shred raw Brussels sprouts. Or, boil in salted water about 5 minutes or until crisp-tender; cut in halves.

Serving ideas—Toss shredded Brussels sprouts in oil-and-vinegar dressing or mayonnaise as for coleslaw.

CABBAGE, CHINESE

Crisp pale-green colored leaves in an elongated head. Sometimes called Napa cabbage in supermarkets.

Preparation—Wash and shred finely; serve raw. The leaves are rather bland.

Serving ideas—Serve with a well-flavored dressing and flavorful ingredients.

CARROTS

Available year around.

Preparation—Coarsely grate raw carrots. Or, serve raw whole baby carrots as part of *Salade de Crudités*, page 20. Slice or dice more mature carrots. If desired, cook in boiling water 10 to 15 minutes, depending on age and size, or until crisp-tender.

Serving ideas—Combine grated carrots, mayonnaise and dried fruits, such as currants and raisins. Toss warm cooked carrots in an oil-and-vinegar dressing made with lemon juice instead of vinegar.

CAULIFLOWER

A flowering cabbage. Available year around; best during cooler months. White is the usual color; but purple ones are occasionally available.

Preparation—Cut into small pieces or divide into flowerets. Serve raw, or boil in salted water 5 minutes or until crisp-tender. Drain; toss with dressing while still warm.

Serving ideas—Serve raw flowerets coated in a spicy dressing or plain as part of *Salade de Crudités*, page 20.

CELERIAC (CELERY ROOT)

The edible root of a special celery variety. It has a mild celery flavor.

Preparation—Peel; toss in lemon juice immediately to prevent discoloration. Grate, shred or dice. Marinate in dressing to soften, or briefly boil shredded or diced celeriac in salted water. Boil shredded celeriac 1 minute; boil diced celeriac 5 minutes. Drain and toss in dressing while warm.

Serving ideas—It is traditionally cut into delicate julienne strips and served in a mustard-mayonnaise mixture. It blends well with carrots in salads.

EGGPLANT

The large purple variety most common; white varieties also available.

Preparation—Trim off stem; cut into slices or dice. These are usually sprinkled with salt. Let drain in a colander 30 minutes to draw out any bitter juices. Rinse and pat dry with paper towels before cooking. Sauté sliced or diced eggplant about 5 minutes or until golden brown and tender. Drain on paper towels. Or, bake whole in a medium oven 30 to 60 minutes, depending on size, or until soft. Or, cook as part of ratatouille, a Provençal vegetable stew.

Serving ideas—Serve sautéed diced or sliced eggplant with a oil-and-vinegar dressing or yogurt dressing. Puree the pulp of baked eggplant to make a dip.

FENNEL

White bulbs with green feathery leaves, a celery-like texture and a slight anise flavor.

Preparation—Slice thinly; serve raw.

Serving ideas—Include as part of *Salade de Crudités*, page 20. Combine with fruit or toss with salad greens.

JÍCAMA

Large, round brown root with a crisp white interior.

Preparation—Peel and slice. Cut slices into strips.

Serving ideas—Add to tossed salads. Or, combine with citrus fruit for an unusual salad.

KOHLRABI

White, pale-green or purple root vegetable. Looks and tastes similar to a turnip.

Preparation—Peel thickly; cut into slices or dice. Cook in boiling salted water 10 to 15 minutes or until tender. Kohlrabi can also be peeled, grated and served raw.

Serving ideas—Toss in oil-and-vinegar dressing.

LEEKS

Large, mild member of the onion family. Can be used whole or sliced, raw or cooked.

Preparation—Wash well to remove all dirt. To eat raw, slice thinly; toss in oil-and-vinegar dressing. Cook whole leeks about 15 minutes in boiling salted water; cook sliced leeks 3 to 5 minutes. Or, poach in stock flavored with a bay leaf, peppercorns, coriander seeds and lemon slices.

Serving ideas—Serve poached leeks at room temperature as a starter. Serve dressed raw leeks as a dinner salad.

LEGUMES

Includes kidney beans, navy beans, black-eyed peas and lentils.

Preparation—Soak overnight in enough water to cover. Or, boil water and beans 5 minutes. Drain soaked beans. Add fresh water; cover and simmer 1 to 2 hours or until tender. Lentils do not need soaking and cook in about 30 minutes. Drain cooked beans or lentils; toss in a parsley-flavored oil-and-vinegar dressing while still warm so that the dressing is absorbed.

Serving ideas—Combine with seafood and butter or margarine for delicious and economical starters. Legumes are a good protein source for vegetarians.

LETTUCE, ENDIVE & OTHER SALAD GREENS

Common varieties of lettuce: leaf, Romaine, Boston or butter and iceberg. The chicory family, with a slightly bitter flavor, includes curly endive, Belgian endive and radicchio. Dandelion leaves, lamb's lettuce, mustard greens, sorrel and watercress can also be used.

Preparation—Wash and dry well. Keep covered in the refrigerator to retain crispness. Dress immediately before serving, or the dressing will wilt the leaves.
Serving ideas—Toss whole or shredded leaves in an herb-flavored dressing.

MUSHROOMS
Available year around. Look for new varieties, such as enoki mushrooms, that are becoming available. Mushrooms are an excellent source of texture and flavor for salads.
Preparation—Wipe with a damp cloth, or rinse quickly in cold running water. Do not peel mushrooms. Use small succulent button mushrooms whole. Slice or chop larger mushrooms.
Serving ideas—Marinate in a lemon dressing; combine with seafood for a delicious starter. Or, try *Lemon & Thyme Mushrooms*, page 54.

PEA PODS, CHINESE
Tender, green peas that are eaten pods and all.
Preparation—If young and tender, trim and serve raw. String more mature pea pods; boil in salted water 1 to 2 minutes or until crisp-tender. Chinese pea pods are also available frozen.
Serving ideas—For a starter, pea pods are especially delicious mixed with shrimp and an oil-and-vinegar dressing made with lemon juice instead of vinegar.

PEPPERS, BELL
Available in green, yellow, red and purple. Red bell peppers are mature green bell peppers; they have a sweeter flavor.
Preparation—Remove stem and seeds. Cut into slices or rings. Or, grill whole peppers until skins blacken and blister. Cool slightly; remove skins. Cut into strips.
Serving ideas—Stuff whole bell peppers; bake until tender. Cool to room temperature. Bell-pepper slices and rings add flavor and texture to salads. Toss warm grilled bell-pepper strips in olive oil. Season with herbs, salt and black pepper. Use bell-pepper strips and rings as garnishes.

SPINACH
Available year around.
Preparation—Prepare as for lettuce. Raw, young, small spinach leaves, tossed in dressing, make a delicious salad. Larger spinach stalks may be cooked and served like asparagus.
Serving ideas—Traditionally served with a hot bacon dressing as a starter. Add to any mixed green salad.

SQUASH, SUMMER (YELLOW & ZUCCHINI)
Preparation—Wash and trim. Cut into thin circles or slice lengthwise. Serve raw, or steam 5 minutes or until crisp-tender.
Serving ideas—Toss in butter, margarine or yogurt dressing.

SUNCHOKES (JERUSALEM ARTICHOKES)
A tuber, resembling a knobby potato, but with the flavor of artichokes.
Preparation—Must be cooked and peeled, either before or after cooking. Place in cold water and lemon juice or vinegar immediately after peeling to prevent browning. Boil in salted water with a little lemon juice or vinegar 10 to 15 minutes or until crisp-tender. Drain and cool.
Serving ideas—Slice and toss in an oil-and-vinegar dressing. Or, combine with mayonnaise, as for potato salad.

New-Potato Salad

1-1/2 lb. medium, new potatoes, scrubbed
2/3 cup Mayonnaise, page 78, or prepared mayonnaise
1 tablespoon white-wine vinegar
2 green onions, chopped
1 tablespoon chopped sweet pickle
1 tablespoon capers, drained
8 small pimento-stuffed olives, thinly sliced
Freshly ground pepper

To garnish:
Pimento-stuffed olives
Sweet pickles

1. In a large saucepan, cover potatoes with cold water. Bring to a boil; simmer 10 to 15 minutes or until tender but not soft. Drain; set aside to cool slightly.
2. Spoon mayonnaise into a large bowl. Stir in vinegar; stir in onions, chopped pickle, capers, sliced olives and pepper.
3. Do not peel potatoes. Leave small potatoes whole; cut larger potatoes into halves or quarters. Add warm potatoes to mayonnaise mixture; stir until coated with dressing. Refrigerate until chilled or up to 24 hours.
4. Spoon into a serving bowl. Garnish with olives and pickles. Serve with a cold-meat selection. Makes 4 dinner salads.

Caribbean Shrimp Salad

1 small head lettuce
2 ripe avocados, peeled, sliced
1 ripe mango, thinly sliced
8 oz. medium shrimp, cooked, peeled, deveined
1/2 cup Thousand Island Dressing, page 78, or prepared
   Thousand Island dressing

To garnish:
2 tablespoons pumpkin seeds, if desired, toasted

1. Wash and dry lettuce; finely shred. Divide shredded lettuce among 4 to 6 salad plates.
2. Arrange avocado and mango slices, slightly overlapping, in a fan shape on lettuce.
3. Spoon dressing into a medium bowl. Stir in shrimp.
4. Spoon shrimp mixture over avocado slices and mango slices. Garnish with pumpkin seeds, if desired. Serve immediately. Makes 4 light main-dish servings or 6 starters.

Variation
Substitute 1 cup seedless green grapes, halved, for mango. Arrange avocado slices over lettuce. Scatter grapes and pumpkin seeds, if desired, over top.

Pineapple & Watercress Salad

1 bunch watercress, trimmed
1 small pineapple
1/3 cup coarsely chopped walnuts

Dressing:
2 tablespoons honey
2 tablespoons olive oil
2 tablespoons white-wine vinegar
Salt
Freshly ground pepper

1. Divide watercress among 4 salad plates.
2. Cut pineapple into 8 slices; peel slices. Cut each peeled slice in half; remove core.
3. Arrange 4 pineapple pieces on each plate; sprinkle with chopped nuts.
4. To make dressing, in a small bowl, combine honey, olive oil and vinegar. Season with salt and pepper; beat with a whisk until blended. Pour dressing over salads. Serve immediately. This is excellent with chicken dishes. Makes 4 dinner salads.

Variation
Substitute 2 peeled, sliced large grapefruit for pineapple.

Top to bottom: Caribbean Shrimp Salad with mango, Caribbean Shrimp Salad with grapes

Smoked-Fish & Bean Salad

1 cup uncooked dried black-eyed peas
Water
1 small onion, finely chopped
1 bay leaf
Freshly ground pepper
2/3 cup Oil & Vinegar Dressing, page 78, or
  prepared dressing
2 teaspoons prepared horseradish
Salt
1 tablespoon chopped fresh parsley
8 oz. smoked mackerel or other smoked fish, skinned,
  flaked
4 hard-cooked eggs, chopped

To serve:
2 or 3 lettuce leaves, if desired
2 lemon slices, twisted
1 or 2 parsley sprigs

---

1. Soak peas overnight in water to cover. Or, boil peas and water 2 minutes. Let stand 1 hour. Drain soaked peas; discard soaking water.
2. In a large saucepan, combine soaked peas, 2-1/2 cups water, onion, bay leaf and pepper. Cover; boil 10 minutes. Reduce heat; simmer 45 minutes to 1 hour or until beans are tender but not mushy. Drain; place in a medium bowl. Cool slightly.
3. In a small bowl, combine dressing, horseradish, salt and chopped parsley. Pour over drained cooled beans; toss gently.
4. Carefully stir fish and hard-cooked eggs into salad. Serve immediately, or cover and refrigerate up to 24 hours.
5. To serve, arrange lettuce in a serving dish or bowl, if desired. Spoon salad over lettuce. Garnish with lemon twists and parsley sprigs. Makes 4 main-dish servings or 6 starters.

Variation
Substitute 1 (15-ounce) can black-eyed peas, drained, for cooked black-eyed peas.

Bouillabaisse Salad

Rouille Mayonnaise:
1-1/4 cups Mayonnaise, page 78, or
  prepared mayonnaise
6 oz. canned pimentos, drained
1 large garlic clove, crushed
1 tablespoon chopped fresh basil, thyme or parsley or
  1-1/2 teaspoons dried leaf basil, thyme or parsley

Salad:
1 onion, coarsely chopped
1 bay leaf
1 bunch fresh parsley or thyme
1 lemon slice or orange slice
Salt
Freshly ground pepper
1-1/4 lb. firm white fish (halibut, turbot or monkfish)
2 medium squid, cleaned
1-1/4 lb. assorted shellfish (mussels, scallops, unpeeled
  shrimp or crayfish tails)

---

1. To make Rouille Mayonnaise, in a small bowl, combine mayonnaise, pimentos, garlic and herbs. If desired, crush pimento, garlic and herbs to a paste in a mortar and pestle. Stir paste into mayonnaise. Cover and store in refrigerator; use within 2 days.
2. To make salad, in a large saucepan, combine 1 quart water, onion, bay leaf, parsley or thyme, lemon slice or orange slice, salt and pepper. Bring to a boil; boil 5 minutes.
3. Cut fish into 2-inch pieces. Add fish pieces to saucepan; simmer 5 to 6 minutes or until fish tests done. Do not overcook. Remove with a slotted spoon; set aside to cool.
4. Cut squid bodies crosswise into 1/4-inch rings. Cut tentacles crosswise in halves or quarters. Add squid pieces to boiling fish-cooking liquid; simmer 15 to 30 seconds or until squid turns opaque. Remove with a slotted spoon; set aside to cool.
5. Add scallops to boiling cooking liquid. Simmer about 5 minutes; remove with a slotted spoon.
6. Add shrimp or crayfish tails to boiling cooking liquid. Simmer 3 minutes or until firm. Remove with a slotted spoon; set aside to cool.
7. Add mussels to boiling cooking liquid; cover pan and simmer 4 to 8 minutes or until shells open. Remove mussels with a slotted spoon; discard any mussels that do not open. Set mussels aside to cool.
8. Place a small decorative bowl in center of a large platter; add mayonnaise. Arrange cooked fish and shellfish around bowl. Leave mussels in bottom shells, as shown.
9. Serve seafood with Rouille Mayonnaise and a green salad. Makes 4 main-dish servings.

Variation
Use any combination of fish and shellfish. Crab, lobster, clams and oysters are popular choices. Frozen shellfish can also be used.

Spring Carrot Salad

1-1/4 lb. small new carrots
Salt
Freshly ground pepper

Dressing:
2/3 cup plain yogurt
Grated peel and juice of 1/2 orange
2 tablespoons chopped fresh parsley or chives
Salt
Freshly ground pepper

This salad relies on the sweet flavor of young spring carrots. It is rich in vitamins and low in calories, making it an excellent choice for dieters.

1. Scrub carrots; leave very small carrots whole. Cut larger carrots in half lengthwise.
2. Place carrots in a medium saucepan. Add 1 cup water; season with salt and pepper. Bring to a boil; simmer 5 to 8 minutes or until carrots are crisp-tender. Drain; set aside to cool.
3. To make dressing, in a small bowl, combine yogurt, orange peel, orange juice and parsley or chives. Season with salt and pepper.
4. Serve immediately, or cover and refrigerate carrots and dressing separately until served. To serve, place cooled carrots on a platter; top with dressing.
5. Serve with cold meats. Makes 4 dinner salads or 6 starters.

Left to right: Bouillabaisse Salad, Smoked-Fish & Bean Salad

Salami, Bean & Tomato Salad

1 cup uncooked dried white beans
Water
1 lb. medium tomatoes (2 or 3)
1 tablespoon chopped fresh sage or 1 teaspoon rubbed
   sage
1 small onion, chopped
4 to 6 oz. thinly sliced salami

Dressing:
1 tablespoon white-wine vinegar
1 tablespoon olive oil
Salt
Freshly ground pepper

To garnish:
1 fresh sage sprig

---

1. Soak beans overnight in water to cover. Or, boil beans
and water 2 minutes. Let stand 1 hour. Drain beans; discard
soaking water.
2. In a large saucepan, combine 2-1/2 cups water and
soaked beans.
3. Peel and chop 1/2 of tomatoes. Add chopped tomatoes
to beans and water; add sage and onion.
4. Bring to a boil. Cover; simmer 1 to 1-1/2 hours or until
tender but not mushy. Drain, reserving 1/3 cup cooking
juice to use in dressing.
5. To make dressing, in a small bowl, combine reserved
cooking liquid, vinegar and olive oil. Season with salt and
pepper. Stir into cooked beans. Serve immediately, or refrigerate up to 24 hours.
6. To serve, arrange overlapping slices of salami around
edge of a serving platter. Thinly slice remaining tomatoes;
arrange tomato slices inside ring of salami slices. Spoon
bean mixture in center of platter. Garnish with a sage
sprig. Makes 4 main-dish servings or 6 to 8 starters.

Variation
Substitute 1 (15-ounce) can white beans for cooked beans.
Drain; reserve 1/3 cup liquid for dressing.

Lentil & Tomato Salad

1 cup uncooked lentils
1 small onion, finely chopped
1 qt. water (4 cups)
1 bay leaf
Salt
6 tablespoons Oil & Vinegar Dressing, page 78, or
   prepared dressing
1 large tomato, chopped
1 small green bell pepper, diced
4 green onions, chopped
8 black olives, if desired, chopped
1 tablespoon chopped fresh parsley

---

1. In a large saucepan, combine lentils, chopped onion,
water, bay leaf and salt. Bring to a boil. Cover; simmer
about 30 minutes or until tender but not mushy.
2. Drain; discard bay leaf. Pour lentil mixture into a salad
bowl. Stir dressing into warm lentil mixture; set aside to
cool. Serve immediately, or cover and refrigerate up to 24
hours.
3. To serve, stir in tomato, bell pepper, green onions and
olives, if desired. Sprinkle with chopped parsley. Makes 4
to 6 dinner salads or 6 to 8 starters.

Left to right: Lentil & Tomato Salad; Salami, Bean & Tomato
Salad; Cracked-Wheat Salad

Cracked-Wheat Salad

1 cup uncooked cracked wheat
1 qt. water (4 cups)
6 tablespoons olive oil
1/4 cup lemon juice
6 tablespoons chopped fresh parsley
2 tablespoons chopped fresh mint or 2 teaspoons
    dried mint
6 green onions, thinly sliced
Salt
Freshly ground pepper

To serve:
1 head lettuce
4 tomatoes, cut into wedges
1 small cucumber, sliced
8 black olives
Parsley or mint sprigs
2 hard-cooked eggs, if desired, quartered

In Lebanon, where this salad originated, preparation is highly individual and quantities of ingredients vary with each family.

1. Soak cracked wheat in water 1 hour. Drain soaked wheat in a sieve; squeeze out any excess water.
2. Pour olive oil and lemon juice into a large bowl. Stir in parsley, mint, onions, salt and pepper. If using dried mint, let stand 15 minutes.
3. Stir drained wheat into dressing until combined. Cover and refrigerate until chilled or up to 24 hours.
4. To serve, arrange lettuce leaves on a serving plate or individual plates. Spoon salad into center of lettuce; garnish with tomatoes, cucumber, olives, parsley or mint sprigs and hard-cooked eggs, if desired. Or, spoon into a large serving bowl. Makes 6 dinner salads or 8 starters.

Salade de Crudités

Salad ingredients:
1 head Bibb lettuce
1 head cauliflower
1/2 cucumber
4 firm tomatoes
1 bunch green onions
1 bunch radishes
8 carrots
12 mushrooms
1 fennel bulb
1 red bell pepper, cut into strips
1 green bell pepper, cut into strips

Dips:
1/2 cup Mayonnaise, page 78
1 cup Hummus, see below
1/2 cup Yogurt Dressing, page 79

1. Clean and trim vegetables. Arrange in a large shallow bowl. Spoon dips into small bowls.
2. Serve with small sharp knives for cutting vegetables as they are eaten with dips. Makes 6 to 8 appetizers.

Hummus

1 cup uncooked garbanzo beans
Water
1/2 cup plain yogurt
2 tablespoons lemon juice
3 tablespoons tahini (sesame-seed paste) or
    peanut butter
1 garlic clove, crushed
Salt
Freshly ground pepper

To serve:
Paprika

1. Soak beans overnight in water to cover. Or, boil beans and water 2 minutes; let stand 1 hour. Drain beans; discard soaking water.
2. In a large saucepan, combine soaked beans and 2 cups water. Cover and boil 10 minutes. Reduce heat; simmer 1 to 1-1/2 hours or until beans are soft enough to mash, adding more water if necessary. Drain; reserve liquid.
3. Mash beans with 2 tablespoons cooking liquid. Beat in yogurt, lemon juice, tahini or peanut butter, garlic, salt and pepper. Or, place all ingredients in a blender or food processor fitted with a steel blade; process until smooth. Thin with an additional cooking liquid if necessary.
4. To serve, sprinkle with paprika; accompany with warm pita bread. Makes 4 main-dish servings or 6 to 8 starters.

Variation
Substitute 1 (15-ounce) can garbanzo beans for cooked beans. Drain; reserve 2 to 4 tablespoons liquid.

Clockwise from left: Pita-bread rounds; Salade de Crudités with Hummus, Mayonnaise and Yogurt Dressing

Spinach & Sardine Mold

1 (10-oz.) pkg. frozen chopped spinach, thawed
1 (1/4-oz.) envelope plus 1/2 teaspoon unflavored
  gelatin powder
1-1/4 cups water
1 chicken-flavored bouillon cube
1 (3-3/4-oz.) can sardines packed in olive oil
3/4 cup dairy sour cream
2 hard-cooked eggs, chopped
Salt
Freshly ground pepper

This is an attractive and unusual way to prepare simple, easily available ingredients. Use a fancy mold to provide a touch of elegance.

1. Squeeze as much liquid as possible from spinach; place in a medium bowl.
2. In a small saucepan, combine gelatin and water. Stir well; let stand 3 minutes. Stir over low heat until gelatin dissolves; stir in bouillon cube until dissolved. Set aside to cool. Pour cooled gelatin mixture over spinach; stir to combine.
3. Place undrained sardines in a small bowl; mash with a fork. Stir mashed sardines into spinach mixture until blended.
4. Fold in sour cream, hard-cooked eggs, salt and pepper. Rinse a 4-cup decorative mold with cold water; drain well. Spoon mixture into mold; smooth top. Refrigerate several hours or until completely set.
5. To serve, insert the tip of a knife around edge of mold. Invert mold on a serving plate. Wet a dish towel with hot water; wring dry. Place hot towel around mold a few seconds. Remove towel and mold. Serve with a tossed salad. Makes 6 to 8 main-dish servings.

Left to right: Spinach & Sardine Mold, Easter-Egg Salad, Curried Vegetable Salad

Curried Vegetable Salad

2 tablespoons vegetable oil
1 medium onion, thinly sliced
1 small apple, peeled, cored, chopped
1 garlic clove, crushed, if desired
1 tablespoon curry powder
1 cup chicken stock
Grated peel of 1/2 lemon
1-1/2 teaspoons lemon juice
6 to 8 new potatoes, scrubbed or peeled
4 carrots, scrubbed or peeled
1/2 head cauliflower, divided into flowerets
2 zucchini, cut into 1/4-inch slices
1/3 cup raisins

To garnish:
1/4 cup sliced almonds
1 tablespoon chopped fresh parsley
Lettuce, if desired
Cold cooked rice, if desired

---

1. Heat oil in a large saucepan over medium heat. Add onion, apple and garlic, if desired; sauté 5 minutes.
2. Stir in curry powder; cook 2 minutes. Stir in stock, lemon peel and lemon juice. Bring to a boil. Reduce heat; simmer 2 minutes.
3. Cut potatoes and carrots into 1/4-inch-wide strips. Add potato and carrot strips to curry sauce. Cover and simmer 10 minutes.
4. Add cauliflower, zucchini and raisins to pan; stir gently. Cover and simmer 6 to 8 minutes or until vegetables are crisp-tender. Cool to room temperature. Serve immediately, or refrigerate up to 24 hours.
5. To serve, toss vegetables gently to coat with curry sauce; spoon into a bowl. Sprinkle with almonds and parsley. Or, serve on lettuce or cold cooked rice. Makes 4 to 6 main-dish servings.

1/To chop parsley, hold knife horizontally; slice across parsley several times.

2/Holding knife by the handle and tip, finely chop parsley with an up-and-down cutting motion.

Easter-Egg Salad

Skins from 2 to 3 large yellow onions
8 eggs
1 head lettuce, shredded
4 oz. bean sprouts (1 cup)
1 cup Green Mayonnaise, page 78, made
    with watercress

To garnish:
1 (4-oz.) jar lumpfish caviar, if desired

For a color contrast, color only half of eggs; leave remaining eggs white.

1. Pour water 3 inches deep into a medium saucepan. Add onion skins to water; bring to a boil. Water will turn a deep golden color.
2. Add eggs to pan; simmer 12 minutes. Remove eggs; reserve cooking liquid. Plunge cooked eggs into cold water.
3. Peel eggs; return to colored water. Simmer 3 minutes or until a rich golden color. Drain; refrigerate until served.
4. To serve, arrange lettuce and bean sprouts on a large plate to resemble a bird's nest. Place hard-cooked eggs on top.
5. Pour some mayonnaise over eggs; serve remaining mayonnaise separately. Garnish with caviar, if desired. Makes 4 main-dish salads or 8 starters.

To make your own bean sprouts, choose unsplit dried beans. Mung beans are the easiest to sprout. Soak 2 tablespoons dried beans in cold water to cover overnight. Drain well; place in a glass jar. Place jar in a cool, dark place. Rinse with room temperature water each morning and evening. Drain beans well after each rinsing to prevent molding. Repeat for 4 days or until sprouts are large enough to use. Mung-bean sprouts are ready to eat when 1 to 2 inches long. Refrigerate sprouts until used. Special perforated, plastic lids are available that fit standard canning jars to make draining easier. Or, cover the tops of the jars with cheesecloth or a piece of a clean nylon stocking; fasten with a elastic band. Alfalfa sprouts can be grown the same way.

Duck, Red-Cabbage & Roquefort Salad

2 large duck breasts, about 1 lb. each
2 tablespoons honey
1/2 head red cabbage
1/2 head lettuce or endive
8 oz. Roquefort cheese
1/4 cup Oil & Vinegar Dressing, page 78, or
   prepared dressing

1. Preheat broiler. Place duck breasts in a baking pan; brush with honey. Cook under preheated broiler about 25 minutes, basting and turning until meat is done and skin is crisp and well-browned. Cool.
2. Slice red cabbage and lettuce or endive thinly; divide among 4 to 6 serving plates.
3. Thinly slice cooled duck; arrange on top of shredded cabbage and lettuce or endive.
4. Cut Roquefort cheese into small cubes; sprinkle over top of salad.
5. Pour 1 tablespoon dressing over each salad immediately before serving. Makes 4 light main-dish servings or 6 starters.

Variation
Substitute 4 small or 2 large chicken breasts for duck.

This recipe is typical of *nouvelle cuisine* cooking where emphasis is on luxurious ingredients, carefully but simply arranged. It is very important that all components be of the best quality and in perfect condition and that extra care be taken in arranging the food.

To preserve the bright color of red cabbage, cut with a stainless-steel knife. If cabbage is cut ahead, toss in vinegar or an oil-and-vinegar dressing to prevent it turning blue.

Roquefort cheese has been produced since ancient time in southwestern France. Its unique and distinct flavor is derived from the humid limestone caves in which it is aged. If you prefer a milder-flavored blue cheese, use Stilton. Domestic blue cheeses are also available.

Ham & Sprouts Salad

2 cartons radish sprouts
4 oz. alfalfa sprouts (1 cup)
8 oz. cooked ham, thinly sliced
4 hard-cooked eggs, chopped

Yogurt-Tartar Dressing:
1/2 cup plain yogurt
1 tablespoon capers
1 tablespoon chopped sweet pickles
1 tablespoon chopped pimento-stuffed olives
1 tablespoon chopped fresh parsley
Salt
Freshly ground pepper

To garnish:
1 carton radish sprouts
2 oz. alfalfa sprouts (1/2 cup), if desired

---

1. In a large bowl, combine radish sprouts and alfalfa sprouts.
2. Cut ham into 2-inch strips; add ham strips and hard-cooked eggs to sprouts. Toss to combine.
3. To make dressing, in a medium bowl, combine all ingredients. Pour dressing over salad; toss salad to coat with dressing.
4. Mound salad in center of a serving platter. Surround with a ring of radish sprouts and alfalfa sprouts, if desired. Serve immediately. Salad is excellent with warm, crusty whole-wheat bread. Makes 4 light main-dish servings.

Chicory & Orange Salad

3 large or 4 small heads Belgian endive
3 medium oranges
1 shallot or small onion, cut in rings
1/4 cup Oil & Vinegar Dressing, page 78, or
   prepared dressing

To garnish:
6 large or 8 small pimento-stuffed olives

---

1. Cut endive crosswise into slices; place in a salad bowl.
2. With a small sharp knife, cut away peel and pith from oranges. Cut into sections, page 30; add to sliced endive. Squeeze any juice remaining in orange membranes into endive mixture.
3. Pour dressing over endive mixture; toss to coat with dressing.
4. Garnish with olives. This is excellent with cold cuts. Makes 4 servings.

Cottage-Cheese Spring Salad

1 lb. cottage cheese (2 cups)
1 tablespoon chopped fresh parsley
1 tablespoon chopped fresh mint or 1-1/2 teaspoons
    dried mint
1 tablespoon chopped chives or green-onion tops, or
    1-1/2 teaspoons dried chives
4 large or 8 small pitted black olives, chopped
Salt
Freshly ground pepper
1 cup diced ham
1 cucumber, diced

To serve:
1 head lettuce or 1 head endive
Black olives
Mint or parsley sprigs

1. Place cottage cheese in a medium bowl. Stir in parsley, mint, chives or green-onion tops and chopped olives. Season with salt and pepper. If using dried herbs, let stand 15 minutes.
2. Stir ham and cucumber into cottage-cheese mixture.
3. Serve immediately, or cover and refrigerate up to 8 hours.
4. To serve, arrange lettuce or endive leaves in a bowl or on a serving platter. Spoon cottage-cheese salad in center; garnish with olives and mint or parsley sprigs. Makes 4 light main-dish servings or 6 starters.

Variation
For special occasions, serve in hollowed-out cucumber boats or in avocado halves.

Left to right: Chicory & Orange Salad; Ham & Sprouts Salad;
Duck, Red-Cabbage & Roquefort Salad

Artichokes Taramasalata

4 artichokes
Salt

Taramasalata:
1 (4-oz.) jar golden caviar
1/2 cup corn oil
1/2 cup plain yogurt
2 tablespoons lemon juice
Freshly ground white pepper
1 garlic clove, if desired, crushed

---

1. Wash artichokes; cut off stalks. As shown below, cut across tops and pull off any outer leaves that are dried or discolored. With kitchen scissors, cut tips from leaves.
2. Cook artichokes, uncovered, in a large pan of boiling salted water 30 to 40 minutes or until done. Artichokes are done when a leaf will pull off easily. Cooking time will depend on size and age of artichokes. Drain artichokes upside down on a plate.
3. To make Taramasalata, place caviar in a medium bowl. Gradually beat oil, yogurt, lemon juice and white pepper into caviar until smooth. Stir in garlic, if desired. Or, place all ingredients in a blender or food processor fitted with a steel blade; process until smooth. Refrigerate until served; mixture will thicken while chilling.
4. When artichokes are cool, remove chokes. To remove chokes, spread top leaves apart; pull out each central cone of small soft leaves. Scoop out and discard chokes, leaving hearts exposed.
5. Spoon Taramasalata into center of artichokes. To eat, pull off an outside leaf; dip fleshy base into Taramasalata. Makes 4 starters.

Salad Sandwiches

4 large rye-bread slices
2 (3-oz.) pkgs. or 1 (8-oz.) pkg. cream cheese,
  room temperature
4 large crisp lettuce leaves
1/4 small cucumber, thinly sliced
4 oz. smoked salmon, sliced

To garnish:
1 carton radish sprouts
Lemon wedges

---

1. Spread bread slices with cheese.
2. Shred lettuce; arrange shredded lettuce on cheese.
3. Arrange cucumber and smoked salmon over lettuce in an attractive pattern.
4. Place open-faced sandwiches on a platter; garnish with radish sprouts and lemon wedges. Makes 4 servings.

Artichoke-Heart Salad

4 cooked medium artichoke hearts
2 oz. mushrooms, thinly sliced
1/4 cup Oil & Vinegar Dressing, page 78, or
  prepared dressing
1 tablespoon chopped fresh parsley or chives
4 bacon slices

---

1. Place artichoke hearts and mushrooms in a serving dish.
2. In a small bowl, combine dressing and herbs; pour over artichoke hearts and mushrooms. Marinate 10 minutes.
3. In a medium skillet, sauté bacon until crisp. Drain on paper towels; cool. Crumble cooled bacon.
4. Immediately before serving, stir chopped bacon into salad. Serve artichokes on individual plates surrounded by mushroom mixture. Makes 4 starters.

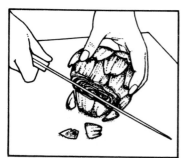
1/Cut across top of artichoke.

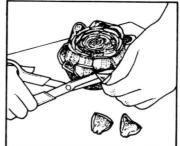
2/With kitchen scissors, cut tips from leaves.

3/Pull out central cone of small soft leaves.

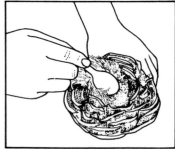
4/Scoop out and discard choke.

Top to bottom: Fresh artichokes, Fresh mushrooms, Artichokes Taramasalata, Artichoke-Heart Salad

Spring Terrine

1/2 lb. lean bacon slices, blanched
1/4 cup butter or margarine
1 medium onion, chopped
1 garlic clove, crushed
1 (10-oz.) pkg. frozen chopped spinach, thawed,
    well drained
1/4 teaspoon freshly grated nutmeg
Salt
Freshly ground pepper
3 eggs
1/4 cup half and half
2 cups fresh bread crumbs
3 tablespoons grated Parmesan cheese
3 hard-cooked eggs

To garnish:
Chicory

---

1. Preheat oven to 350F (175C). Line bottom and long sides of an 8" x 4" or 7" x 3" loaf pan with bacon slices. Overlap slices slightly; drape ends over sides of pan.
2. Melt butter or margarine in a large skillet. Add onion and garlic; sauté until onion is transparent. Stir in spinach; cook 2 minutes. Season with nutmeg, salt and pepper. Set aside to cool slightly.
3. In another medium bowl, beat eggs and half and half until blended; stir in spinach mixture. Stir in bread crumbs and cheese until blended. Spoon 1/3 of spinach mixture into bottom of bacon-lined pan. Arrange hard-cooked eggs down center of spinach mixture. Spoon remaining spinach mixture into pan, covering eggs completely. Fold bacon slices over spinach filling; cover pan with foil.
4. Bake in preheated oven 1 hour 10 minutes. Remove foil; bake 10 minutes or until spinach filling is firm. Drain off fat; place pan on a wire rack to cool. Refrigerate if not served immediately. Bring to room temperature before serving.
5. To serve, invert terrine on a serving plate; remove mold. Garnish with chicory. Cut into 6 to 8 slices. Makes 6 to 8 servings.

Asparagus Mousse

1 lb. fresh asparagus
1-1/2 cups water
Milk
2 tablespoons butter or margarine
2 tablespoons all-purpose flour
1 (1/4-oz.) envelope plus 1 teaspoon unflavored
    gelatin powder
1/4 cup cold water
Grated peel of 1/2 lemon
1 tablespoon lemon juice
1 hard-cooked egg, chopped
2/3 cup plain yogurt
Salt
Freshly ground white pepper

---

1. Wash asparagus; snap off and discard tough woody ends. Cut off stalks 1-1/2 inches below tips. Reserve stalks. Bring 1-1/2 cups water to a boil in a medium saucepan. Add asparagus tips; cook 6 to 8 minutes or until crisp-tender. Remove with a slotted spoon; set aside to cool. When cool, cover and refrigerate for garnish.
2. Chop reserved stalks; add to water in saucepan. Cover and cook 10 to 15 minutes or until soft. Drain stalks, reserving cooking liquid. Set stalks aside.
3. Pour cooking liquid into a 2-cup measuring cup; add enough milk to make 2 cups. Set aside. Melt butter or margarine in a medium saucepan. Stir in flour; cook over low heat 1 minute. Gradually stir in reserved cooking-liquid mixture; cook, stirring constantly, until mixture is thickened and comes to a boil. Add reserved stalks; cook 1 minute. Remove from heat; pour into a medium bowl.
4. In a small saucepan, combine gelatin and 1/4 cup water. Stir well; let stand 3 minutes. Stir over low heat until gelatin dissolves. Stir into cooled asparagus mixture. Set aside to cool.
5. Stir lemon peel, lemon juice, hard-cooked egg and yogurt into asparagus mixture until blended. Season with salt and white pepper. Rinse a 4- to 4-1/2-cup decorative mold in cold water. Pour in asparagus mixture; refrigerate several hours or until set.
6. To serve, insert the tip of a knife around edge of mold. Invert mold on a serving plate. Wet a dish towel with hot water; wring dry. Wrap hot towel around mold a few seconds. Remove towel and mold. Garnish with reserved asparagus tips. Makes 6 to 8 servings.

Variation
Substitute 2 (10-ounce) packages frozen asparagus spears for fresh asparagus. Cook according to package directions; cool. Cut off stalks to use in mousse. Reserve tips for garnish.

Left to right: Fresh asparagus, Asparagus Mousse, Spring Terrine

Wilted Spinach Salad

8 oz. fresh, young spinach leaves (about 4 cups)
4 bacon slices, chopped
1 small garlic clove, if desired, crushed
1 tablespoon lemon juice

1. Wash spinach thoroughly; remove coarse stalks. Drain; pat leaves dry with paper towels. Leave smaller leaves whole; shred larger leaves. Place spinach in a large bowl.
2. To make dressing, combine bacon and garlic in a large skillet. Cook 5 minutes or until bacon is browned and crisp, stirring occasionally.
3. Remove from heat; carefully pour in lemon juice to avoid spatters. Stir quickly. Add spinach while dressing is still hot. Toss until all leaves are coated and have begun to wilt. Makes 4 dinner salads.

Summer

Chicken, Tarragon & Orange Salad

1 (2-1/2-lb.) broiler-fryer chicken
1 medium onion, thinly sliced
Grated peel and juice of 1 orange
1 tablespoon chopped fresh tarragon or 1-1/2 teaspoons
    dried leaf tarragon
1 bay leaf
Water
Salt
Freshly ground pepper
1 tablespoon vegetable oil
1/2 to 1 tablespoon white-wine vinegar

To garnish:
1 small orange, peeled, sliced
1 carton radish sprouts
Fresh tarragon sprigs, if desired

1. Place chicken, onion, orange peel, orange juice, tarragon and bay leaf in a large saucepan.
2. Add enough water to almost cover chicken; season with salt and pepper. Cover; bring to a boil. Reduce heat; simmer 45 minutes to 1 hour or until chicken is tender.
3. Lift out chicken; let cool. Discard bay leaf and onion.
4. Boil cooking liquid until reduced to 1 cup. Let cool; refrigerate until chilled.
5. When chicken is cool, remove meat from bones, discarding skin and bones. Cut meat into bite-size pieces; place in a medium bowl. Refrigerate while stock is chilling.
6. When stock is chilled, remove fat layer from top. Reheat stock; stir in oil and vinegar to taste. Pour over chicken pieces; toss well.
7. Serve at once, or cover and refrigerate up to 24 hours. To serve, spoon into a serving dish; garnish with orange slices, sprouts and tarragon sprigs, if desired. Makes 4 main-dish servings.

Lettuce & Orange Salad with Almond Dressing

1 head iceberg lettuce
2 oranges
1/2 cup vegetable oil
1/2 cup slivered blanched almonds
1 tablespoon lemon juice
Salt
Freshly ground pepper

1. Tear lettuce into pieces; place in a salad bowl.
2. Remove peel and white pith from oranges; section peeled oranges. See box below. Add orange sections to lettuce pieces; squeeze orange juice from membranes over top.
3. Heat oil in a medium saucepan over medium heat. Add almonds; sauté, stirring constantly, about 3 minutes or until golden brown.
4. Cool almonds slightly; stir in lemon juice, salt and pepper.
5. Pour almond mixture over lettuce and orange segments; toss until well coated.
6. Serve immediately. Makes 4 to 6 dinner salads.

To make orange sections, cut a slice off top and bottom of an orange. Place orange on a cutting board. With a small serrated knife, make smooth downward cuts, following the curve of the orange. When all peel is removed, check that all white pith has also been removed. Cut away any remaining pith. To make sections, hold orange in the palm of one hand; with a sharp paring knife, cut down on either side of each membrane to the center of orange to free sections. Carefully lift out sections.

Top to bottom: Lettuce & Orange Salad with Almond Dressing; Chicken, Tarragon & Orange Salad

Caesar Salad

5 tablespoons corn oil or olive oil
1 garlic clove, crushed
2 thick bread slices, cut into 1/2-inch cubes
1 head Romaine lettuce
1 (2-oz.) can anchovy fillets
1/4 cup grated Parmesan cheese
1 tablespoon lemon juice
Salt
Freshly ground pepper
1 egg

1. To make croutons, heat 2 tablespoons corn oil or olive oil in a medium skillet over medium heat. Add garlic and bread cubes; sauté until bread is crisp and golden brown. Drain on paper towels.
2. Tear or cut lettuce into bite-size pieces; place lettuce pieces into a salad bowl.
3. Chop anchovy fillets; add chopped anchovies and their oil to lettuce. Add Parmesan cheese; toss to combine.
4. Add remaining corn oil or olive oil, lemon juice, salt and pepper; toss well.
5. Cook egg in a small saucepan of boiling water 1 minute. Break egg over salad; toss gently. Add croutons; toss to combine. Makes 4 dinner salads or 4 to 6 starters.

Italian Tomato Salad

6 small tomatoes, thinly sliced
6 oz. sliced Mozzarella cheese
10 to 12 small black olives

Dressing:
1/4 cup olive oil
1-1/2 tablespoons white-wine vinegar
2 tablespoons chopped fresh basil or 2 teaspoons
   dried leaf basil
Salt
Freshly ground pepper

1. Arrange sliced tomatoes in a shallow serving dish.
2. Place cheese slices in center of tomatoes, so that tomatoes are visible around edge of dish; see photo.
3. Arrange olives on tomatoes.
4. To make dressing, in a small bowl, combine olive oil, vinegar, basil, salt and pepper. If using dried basil, let dressing stand 15 minutes.
5. Pour dressing over tomatoes, cheese and olives. Serve immediately, or refrigerate 2 to 3 hours. Makes 4 dinner salads or 6 starters.

Left to right: Caesar Salad, Italian Tomato Salad,
Pipérade-Stuffed Tomatoes, Greek Salad with Tahini Dressing

Pipérade-Stuffed Tomatoes

4 large tomatoes
1/4 cup butter or margarine
2 bacon slices, chopped
1 shallot, finely chopped
1 small red or green bell pepper, diced
4 eggs, slightly beaten
Salt
Freshly ground black pepper

To serve:
1 small head lettuce

---

1. Slice tops off tomatoes; reserve for lids.
2. Scoop out centers of tomatoes with a grapefruit knife or spoon. Chop centers; set aside. Place tomato cases, cut-side down, on a plate to drain.
3. Melt 2 tablespoons butter or margarine in a medium saucepan. Add bacon, shallot and bell pepper; sauté 5 minutes.
4. Add chopped tomatoes; simmer 10 minutes or until reduced to a thick puree, stirring occasionally.
5. In another saucepan, melt remaining butter or margarine over medium heat; pour in eggs. Cook gently, stirring with a wooden spoon, until eggs are scrambled.
6. Stir tomato mixture into scrambled eggs; season with salt and pepper. Cool to room temperature.
7. Fill tomato cases with cool mixture; replace lids. Separate lettuce into leaves; arrange lettuce leaves on a serving plate. Place stuffed tomatoes on lettuce. Makes 4 main-dish servings or 4 starters.

Greek Salad with Tahini Dressing

1/2 large cucumber
3 small tomatoes, cut into thin wedges
1 small green bell pepper, sliced
1 small onion, thinly sliced
8 small pitted black olives, halved
4 oz. feta cheese

Tahini Dressing:
2 tablespoons tahini paste
1/4 cup plain yogurt
1 to 2 tablespoons water
2 tablespoons chopped fresh parsley
1 small garlic clove, if desired, crushed
Salt
Freshly ground pepper

---

1. Cut cucumber into 1/4-inch slices; cut slices into 1/4-inch-wide strips. Place cucumber strips into a salad bowl.
2. Add tomatoes, bell pepper, onion and olives. Cube feta cheese; set aside.
3. To make dressing, spoon tahini paste into a small bowl. Slowly beat in yogurt; thin with water if necessary. Stir in parsley and garlic, if desired. Season with salt and pepper.
4. Pour dressing over salad; toss well. Sprinkle cheese cubes over salad. Serve immediately.
5. This is excellent with cold roasted meats and pita bread. Makes 4 to 6 dinner salads.

Mediterranean Bean Salad

1 lb. fresh green beans
Salt

Dressing:
6 tablespoons olive oil
Grated peel of 1 small lemon
2 tablespoons lemon juice
2 hard-cooked eggs, chopped
8 small black olives
1 small garlic clove, if desired, crushed
Salt
Freshly ground pepper

1. Trim and string beans. If beans are small, leave whole; cut beans in half crosswise, if large.
2. Place prepared beans and a little salt in a saucepan. Add enough boiling water to almost cover; simmer about 10 minutes or until crisp-tender.
3. Drain beans; rinse with cold water to cool quickly.
4. To make dressing, pour olive oil into a serving bowl large enough to hold beans. Stir in lemon peel, lemon juice, hard-cooked eggs, olives and garlic, if desired. Season with salt and pepper.
5. Add cooled beans to dressing; toss to coat beans with dressing. Serve immediately, or refrigerate several hours. Makes 4 dinner salads or 6 starters.

Variation
For a richer Mediterranean flavor, add 1 (2-ounce) can anchovy fillets, chopped, with cooled beans.

Bean & Bacon Salad

1 lb. shelled green lima beans or broad beans
   (about 2 cups)
1/2 cup plain yogurt
2 tablespoons chopped fresh parsley
1 teaspoon dried leaf oregano
1 tablespoon finely chopped onion
Salt
Freshly ground pepper

To garnish:
4 crisp-cooked bacon slices, crumbled

1. If using broad beans, remove skins. Place beans in a medium saucepan. Add enough boiling water to cover. Simmer lima beans about 15 minutes or until tender. Broad beans need 25 to 30 minutes. Drain cooked beans; rinse with cold water to cool quickly.
2. To make dressing, in a small bowl, combine yogurt, parsley, oregano and onion; season with salt and pepper.
3. Place cooled beans into a serving bowl; stir dressing into beans. Sprinkle with bacon. Serve immediately, or refrigerate several hours. Makes 4 to 6 dinner salads.

Pasta & Pesto Salad

8 oz. uncooked pasta, any shape (about 2 cups)
Salt

Pesto:
1/2 cup fresh basil leaves, chopped
1/4 cup grated Parmesan cheese
1 garlic clove, crushed
About 6 tablespoons olive oil
1 tablespoon lemon juice
Salt
Freshly ground pepper
1/4 cup pine nuts or chopped blanched almonds

1. Cook pasta in a large saucepan of boiling salted water according to package directions until tender. Do not overcook.
2. Drain cooked pasta; rinse with cold water to cool quickly.
3. To make Pesto, place basil in a bowl large enough to hold pasta. Add cheese, garlic, 6 tablespoons olive oil, lemon juice, salt and pepper. Beat until blended. Or, place ingredients in a blender or food processor fitted with a steel blade; process until smooth.
4. Stir in pine nuts or almonds. Add cooled pasta; toss until pasta is coated with dressing. If pasta seems dry, add additional oil. Serve immediately, or cover and refrigerate up to 24 hours. Serve with ham or other cold meats. Makes 4 to 6 dinner salads.

Variation
If fresh basil is not available, substitute 1/4 cup chopped fresh parsley and 2 tablespoons dried leaf basil for fresh basil.

Clockwise from left: Mediterranean Bean Salad, Pasta & Pesto Salad, Bean & Bacon Salad

Salmon with Cucumber Sauce

4 salmon steaks, about 6 oz. each
Salt
Freshly ground pepper
1 lemon
4 parsley or dill sprigs
1/4 cup dry white wine or water

Cucumber Sauce:
1 cucumber, about 10 inches long
1/2 cup Mayonnaise, page 78, or prepared mayonnaise

To serve:
1 lettuce heart
Dill or parsley sprigs

---

1. Preheat oven to 350F (175C). Grease a baking dish large enough to hold salmon in a single layer. Place salmon steaks in greased baking dish; season with salt and pepper.
2. Grate peel from lemon; reserve for sauce. Cut lemon into thin slices; place 1 slice on each steak.
3. Place 1 parsley or dill sprig on each salmon steak; add wine or water. Cover with a lid or foil.
4. Bake in preheated oven 10 to 15 minutes or until salmon tests done. Set aside to cool; reserve cooking liquid.
5. To make sauce, dice cucumber. Place diced cucumber in a small bowl. Stir mayonnaise and reserved salmon cooking liquid into cucumber. Stir in reserved lemon peel, salt and pepper.
6. To serve, carefully remove skin and center bones from salmon, keeping steaks whole. Discard baked lemon slices and parsley or dill. Arrange steaks on a serving plate. Spoon sauce down center of each baked salmon where bone has been removed. Garnish with lettuce and a dill or parsley sprig. Serve immediately. Makes 4 main-dish servings.

Variation
Substitute halibut, turbot or cod for salmon. If dill is not available, substitute the feathery leaves from fennel.

Seafood-Stuffed Lettuce

1 large head lettuce
4 hard-cooked eggs, chopped
8 oz. shrimp, cooked, peeled, deveined
6 oz. cooked crabmeat
1/2 cup Anchovy Mayonnaise, page 78
1 tablespoon lemon juice
2 tablespoons chopped fresh chives
2 tablespoons chopped fresh parsley
Salt
Freshly ground pepper

---

1. Remove and discard outside leaves from lettuce; keep remaining leaves attached. Carefully wash lettuce; shake to remove excess water. Invert on paper towels or a clean dish towel.
2. To make stuffing, in a medium bowl, combine hard-cooked eggs, shrimp and crabmeat. Stir in Anchovy Mayonnaise, lemon juice, chives and parsley. Season with salt and pepper. Stuffing can be made several hours in advance; refrigerate until served. Stuff lettuce immediately before serving.
3. To serve, place lettuce on a large plate. Gently pull apart center leaves; remove lettuce heart.
4. Spoon stuffing into center of lettuce. Makes 4 main-dish servings or 6 to 8 starters.

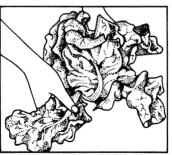
1/Remove and discard outside leaves from lettuce.

2/Remove lettuce heart.

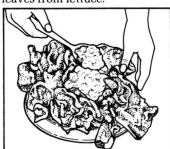
3/Spoon stuffing into center of lettuce.

Eggplant Salad

1 (1-1/4-lb.) eggplant
1 tablespoon salt
5 tablespoons olive oil
1 medium onion, chopped
1 garlic clove, crushed
2 large tomatoes
1/2 cup chopped walnuts

Dressing:
1 tablespoon chopped fresh basil or 1-1/2 teaspoons
    dried leaf basil
1/2 cup Yogurt Dressing, page 79
Salt
Freshly ground pepper

To garnish:
1 tablespoon chopped fresh parsley

1. Cut eggplant into 1/2-inch cubes; place eggplant cubes in a colander. Sprinkle with salt; shake to distribute salt over all cubes. Place colander on a plate to drain; let stand 1 hour. Rinse; pat dry with paper towels.
2. Heat olive oil in a large skillet. Add rinsed eggplant, onion and garlic. Cook over medium heat 10 minutes or until eggplant is tender and browned, stirring frequently. Set aside to cool.
3. Spoon cooked eggplant mixture into a medium bowl. Dice tomatoes; stir diced tomatoes and walnuts into eggplant mixture.
4. To make dressing, in a small bowl, stir basil into Yogurt Dressing. Season with salt and pepper. Stir seasoned dressing into eggplant mixture until combined.
5. Spoon salad into a serving bowl; sprinkle with parsley. Serve immediately, or cover and refrigerate up to 24 hours. Bring to room temperature before serving. Makes 4 to 6 dinner salads.

Left to right: Salmon with Cucumber Sauce, Seafood-Stuffed Lettuce

Midsummer Salad

1 small ripe melon, such as cantaloupe or honeydew
3/4 cup strawberries, hulled
1 (3-inch) cucumber piece
1 small head leaf lettuce, shredded

Mint Dressing:
1/4 cup Oil & Vinegar Dressing, page 78, or
    prepared dressing
2 tablespoons chopped fresh mint
Salt
Freshly ground pepper

To garnish:
2 tablespoons slivered almonds

1. Cut melon into quarters; remove and discard seeds and skin. Scoop into balls with a melon baller, or cut into 1/2-inch cubes.
2. Cut strawberries and cucumber into thin slices.
3. To serve, arrange lettuce on a large serving plate or 4 individual plates. Arrange melon balls or cubes, strawberry slices and cucumber slices over lettuce.
4. In a small bowl, combine oil-and-vinegar dressing, mint, salt and pepper. Pour over salad immediately before serving; sprinkle with almonds. Serve with a selection of hard and soft cheeses or ham. Makes 4 dinner salads or 4 to 6 starters.

Variations
Serve salad in small melon halves instead of plates. Substitute banana slices or kiwifruit slices for some or all of strawberries.

Peperonata

2 tablespoons olive oil
1 large onion, sliced
4 to 6 red and green bell peppers, quartered
1 garlic clove, if desired, crushed
4 to 5 small tomatoes, peeled
Salt
Freshly ground black pepper

1. Heat olive oil in a large skillet. Add onion; sauté 5 minutes.
2. Cut bell peppers into 1/4-inch slices; add bell-pepper slices and garlic, if desired, to skillet. Cover skillet; simmer 10 minutes.
3. Cut each tomato into 8 wedges; add tomato wedges to bell-pepper mixture. Season with salt and black pepper.
4. Simmer, uncovered, 15 to 20 minutes or until vegetables are tender, stirring occasionally. Tomatoes should be tender but still hold their shape.
5. Spoon cooked vegetables and their juice into a serving bowl; cool to room temperature. Makes 4 dinner salads or 6 to 8 starters.

Clockwise from top: Midsummer Salad with Mint Dressing, Selection of cheeses, Zucchini-Timbale Salad

Zucchini-Timbale Salad

1-1/2 lb. zucchini, trimmed, cut into
    1/2-inch thick slices
Salt
1 tablespoon freshly chopped basil or 1-1/2 teaspoons
    dried leaf basil
4 eggs
2/3 cup half and half
Freshly ground pepper
2 tablespoons grated Parmesan cheese

To serve:
3 to 4 tomatoes, sliced
1 carton radish sprouts
6 tablespoons Oil & Vinegar Dressing, page 78, or
    prepared dressing

1. Preheat oven to 350F (175C). Grease 6 (3/4-cup) ramekins.
2. Cook zucchini in a medium saucepan of lightly salted boiling water 5 minutes. Drain well; set aside to cool. In a blender or food processor fitted with a steel blade, process cooled zucchini and basil until smooth. Pour puree into a medium bowl.
3. In a small bowl, beat eggs and half and half until blended. Stir into zucchini puree until blended. Season with salt and pepper.
4. Spoon zucchini mixture into greased ramekins. Place filled ramekins on a baking sheet; sprinkle 1 teaspoon cheese over top of each ramekin.
5. Bake in preheated oven 45 to 50 minutes or until set. Remove from baking sheet; cool completely on a wire rack. Refrigerate timbales in ramekins until served.
6. To serve, run the tip of a knife around edge of each ramekin; invert ramekins on individual serving plates. Remove ramekins. Cut tomato slices in half; arrange around each timbale. Garnish with radish sprouts. Spoon 1 tablespoon dressing over each timbale. Makes 6 light main-dish servings.

Marinated Mackerel

4 medium mackerel, ready to cook
1/2 cup white wine or apple juice
1/2 cup water
1 lemon slice
1 large parsley sprig
1 large thyme sprig or 1 teaspoon dried leaf thyme
1 bay leaf
Salt
Freshly ground pepper

To garnish:
1 tablespoon chopped fresh parsley
1 tablespoon chopped fresh chives
Shredded lettuce or cucumber slices

1. Preheat oven to 350F (175C). Place fish in a baking pan. Add wine or apple juice, water, lemon, herbs, salt and pepper. Cover with a lid or foil.
2. Bake in preheated oven 20 minutes or until fish tests done.
3. Set aside to cool. When fish is cool, remove and discard skin.
4. Pour cooking liquid into a small saucepan; boil until reduced to about 1/2 cup.
5. Place cooled fish in a shallow serving dish; add reduced cooking liquid. Cover and refrigerate until chilled.
6. To serve, sprinkle with chopped parsley and chives; garnish with lettuce or cucumber. Makes 4 main-dish salads.

Beet & Orange Salad

1 (1-lb.) can cut beets, drained
1 medium orange
1/2 cup dairy sour cream
2 tablespoons chopped fresh chives
Salt
Freshly ground pepper

1. Arrange beets in a shallow serving dish.
2. Grate peel from 1/2 of orange; cut orange in half. Squeeze juice from grated orange half. Set orange peel and orange juice aside. Cut peel and white pith from remaining orange half; cut peeled orange half into sections. Scatter orange sections over beets.
3. In a small bowl, combine orange peel, orange juice and sour cream. Stir in chives, salt and pepper. Pour dressing over beets and orange; do not stir. Serve immediately. Makes 4 dinner salads.

French Lamb Salad

1 lb. cold roast lamb, preferably medium rare
1/4 cup olive oil
2 tablespoons white-wine vinegar
2 tablespoons chopped fresh mint or 1 tablespoon dried leaf mint
Salt
Freshly ground pepper
4 green onions, chopped
1 cup cooked green peas

To serve:
1 head lettuce
Mint sprigs

1. Cut lamb into 3/4-inch cubes.
2. To make dressing, pour oil into a bowl large enough to hold lamb and vegetables. Whisk in vinegar, mint, salt and pepper.
3. Stir in lamb cubes and green onions until coated with dressing. Gently stir in peas. Serve immediately, or cover and refrigerate up to 24 hours.
4. Immediately before serving, shred lettuce; stir shredded lettuce into lamb salad. Spoon into a serving dish; garnish with mint sprigs. Makes 4 main-dish servings.

Zucchini Ratatouille

2 tablespoons olive oil
1 medium onion, thinly sliced
1 garlic clove, crushed
1 lb. zucchini, sliced
2 or 3 small tomatoes, peeled, sliced
1 small eggplant, diced
1 green bell pepper, cut into thin strips
1 tablespoon chopped fresh oregano or 1-1/2 teaspoons
    dried leaf oregano
Salt
Freshly ground black pepper

To garnish:
1 tablespoon chopped fresh parsley

This dish originates from Provence in southern France. Serve hot or at room temperature. The flavor is even better if prepared the day before serving.

1. Heat olive oil in a large saucepan. Add onion and garlic; sauté 5 minutes.
2. Add zucchini, tomatoes, eggplant and bell pepper to pan. Sprinkle with oregano, salt and black pepper; stir gently.
3. Cover and simmer 10 to 15 minutes or until vegetables are tender but hold their shapes. Cool to room temperature. Serve immediately, or cover and refrigerate up to 24 hours. Bring to room temperature before serving.
4. To serve, turn into a serving dish; sprinkle with chopped parsley. Serve with grilled meats. Makes 4 dinner salads.

Left to right: Beet & Orange Salad, Marinated Mackerel

Seafood Mousse

1 lb. white fish fillets
2/3 cup dry white wine
2/3 cup water
1 small onion, sliced
1 thick lemon slice
1 bay leaf
Parsley sprigs
Salt
6 peppercorns
Milk
2 tablespoons butter or margarine
2-1/2 tablespoons all-purpose flour
1/4 cup cold water
1 (1/4-oz.) envelope plus 1 teaspoon unflavored gelatin
  powder
1 tablespoon lemon juice
1 teaspoon anchovy paste
1 teaspoon paprika
1/2 pint dairy sour cream (1 cup)
1 egg, separated
Freshly ground white pepper

To garnish:
Thinly sliced cucumbers
1 carton radish sprouts
Green Mayonnaise, page 78

1. Preheat oven to 350F (175C). Place fish in a shallow baking dish. Add wine, 2/3 cup water, onion, lemon, bay leaf, parsley, salt and peppercorns. Cover with a lid or foil.
2. Bake in preheated oven 20 minutes or until fish tests done. Let cool slightly. Remove fish with a slotted spoon; set aside. Strain cooking liquid into a 2-cup measuring cup; add enough milk to make 2 cups. Set aside.
3. Melt butter or margarine in a medium saucepan. Stir in flour; cook over low heat 1 minute. Gradually stir in cooking liquid and milk; cook, stirring constantly, until sauce is thickened and comes to a boil. Lower heat; simmer 2 minutes, stirring occasionally. Set aside to cool.
4. Flake fish into a large bowl; mash with a fork. Stir in sauce until blended. In a small saucepan, combine 1/4 cup water and gelatin. Stir well; let stand 3 minutes. Stir over low heat until gelatin dissolves. Stir into fish mixture.
5. Stir in lemon juice, anchovy paste, paprika, sour cream and egg yolk until thoroughly blended. In a small bowl, beat egg white until stiff peaks form; fold into fish mixture. Season with salt and white pepper.
6. Rinse a 5- to 5-1/2-cup decorative fish mold with cold water. Pour in fish mixture; refrigerate several hours or until set.
7. To serve, run the tip of a knife around edge of mold. Invert mold on a large serving plate. Wet a dish towel with hot water; wring dry. Wrap hot towel around mold for a few seconds. Remove towel and mold. Garnish mousse with cucumber slices and radish sprouts. Serve with Green Mayonnaise. Makes 8 to 10 main-dish servings.

Seafood Mousse

Oriental Pea-Pod Salad

1-1/4 lb. Chinese pea pods
Salt
4 oz. mushrooms, thinly sliced
1 small red bell pepper, finely chopped
8 oz. shrimp, cooked, peeled, deveined

Dressing:
3 tablespoons vegetable oil
1 tablespoon soy sauce
1 to 2 tablespoons lemon juice
1 teaspoon brown or white sugar, if desired

To garnish:
2 tablespoons sesame seeds

1. String pea pods, if necessary. Place in a medium sauce-pan of boiling salted water. Return to a boil; simmer 1 minute. Drain immediately; rinse with cold water to cool quickly. Drain again.
2. Combine drained pea pods, mushrooms, bell pepper and shrimp in a medium bowl.
3. To make dressing, in a small bowl, combine oil, soy sauce and lemon juice to taste. Stir in sugar until dissolved if a sweet dressing is desired.
4. Pour dressing over shrimp mixture; toss to coat with dressing. Cover and refrigerate up to 8 hours.
5. To serve, spoon into a large serving bowl or individual serving bowls; sprinkle with sesame seeds. Makes 4 light main-dish servings or 6 to 8 starters.

Variation

Substitute sugar peas for Chinese pea pods. Sugar peas look like swollen pea pods. Do not cook; they are tender and deliciously sweet.

Cucumber Salad with Dill

1 large cucumber
1 tablespoon salt

Dressing:
1/4 cup white-wine vinegar
1 tablespoon sugar
1 tablespoon chopped fresh dill or 1-1/2 teaspoons
   dried dill weed
Freshly ground pepper

To garnish:
1 tablespoon chopped fresh dill or parsley

This refreshing Scandinavian salad is best made a day ahead. It is an excellent choice for a summer buffet party, especially one which has salmon on the menu.

1. Score cucumber skin by running prongs of a fork down its length, all the way around.
2. Thinly slice cucumber with a sharp knife or a food processor fitted with a slicing attachment.
3. Place cucumber slices in a colander or sieve; sprinkle with salt. Shake to distribute salt over all slices. Place colander in a bowl to drain.
4. Let stand 1 to 2 hours, shaking occasionally, or until about 1/2 cup of liquid has drained off.
5. Rinse cucumber in cold water to remove excess salt; drain well on paper towels. Place drained cucumber in a shallow serving dish.
6. To make dressing, in a small bowl, combine all ingredients. Pour dressing over cucumber slices. Refrigerate until chilled or up to 24 hours.
7. To serve, sprinkle with chopped dill or parsley. Serve with cold salmon or other fish dishes. Makes 4 servings.

Variation

Tzatziki: To make this refreshing Greek salad, substitute a mint-and-yogurt dressing for the dill dressing. To make mint-and-yogurt dressing, add 1-1/2 teaspoons dried leaf mint or 1 tablespoon fresh chopped mint to Yogurt Dressing, page 79.

Top to bottom: Oriental Pea-Pod Salad, Country Salad

Zucchini & Mint Salad

1-1/2 lb. zucchini
2 teaspoons salt
1/2 cup pine nuts or slivered almonds
2/3 cup raisins

Dressing:
6 tablespoons olive oil
2 tablespoons lemon juice
2 tablespoons chopped fresh mint
Freshly ground pepper

---

1. Wash zucchini; coarsely grate into a colander. Sprinkle with salt; shake to distribute salt evenly. Place colander in a bowl to drain. Let stand about 1 hour to drain off excess juices. Rinse in cold water to remove excess salt. Drain and pat dry with paper towels.
2. Place drained zucchini in a medium bowl; stir in pine nuts or almonds and raisins.
3. To make dressing, in a small bowl, combine all ingredients; pour over zucchini mixture. Toss to combine. Serve immediately.
4. Serve with cold roasted lamb or chicken. Makes 4 dinner salads.

Country Salad

1 small head lettuce
1 bunch dandelion leaves or 1/2 head curly endive
8 oz. lamb's lettuce
1 small bunch chives
1/2 cup Yogurt & Blue-Cheese Dressing, page 79, or
   prepared blue-cheese dressing

---

1. Wash lettuce; dry. Shred coarsely. Place shredded lettuce in a salad bowl.
2. Wash dandelion leaves, removing coarse stalks; dry. Add to lettuce.
3. Wash lamb's lettuce; dry. Separate into sprigs; add to lettuce mixture.
4. Chop chives; add to lettuce mixture.
5. Pour dressing over salad; toss to coat salad with dressing. Makes 4 dinner salads.

Pears with Blue Cheese

2/3 cup plain yogurt
4 oz. Stilton cheese or other blue cheese,
  room temperature
Freshly ground pepper
1 small head lettuce
4 ripe pears

To garnish:
1 bunch watercress

1. In a small bowl, blend yogurt and 2 ounces cheese until smooth. Season with pepper.
2. Arrange lettuce leaves on 4 individual plates. Core and slice pears, arranging 1 pear on each plate.
3. Spoon dressing over pear slices. Crumble remaining cheese; sprinkle over dressing.
4. Garnish each plate with a few watercress sprigs. Serve immediately. Makes 4 dinner salads or 4 starters.

Variation
For a more substantial salad, add 1 small ham slice to each serving.

Peaches & Cream Salad

1 (8-oz.) pkg. cream cheese, room temperature
1 to 2 tablespoons half and half or milk
Salt
Freshly ground pepper
1 cup chopped mixed nuts, toasted
Lettuce leaves
4 ripe peaches or nectarines, halved, pitted

1. In a medium bowl, beat cheese until smooth; thin with half and half or milk, if necessary. Season with salt and pepper. Stir in 1/2 cup nuts.
2. Divide lettuce leaves among 4 individual plates; place 2 peach or nectarine halves on each plate.
3. Spoon some cream-cheese filling into center of each peach or nectarine half; sprinkle with remaining nuts. Makes 4 starters.

Variation
Pineapple & Cream Cheese: Substitute 4 fresh or canned pineapple slices for peaches or nectarines. Mound cream-cheese mixture in center of slices.

Melon & Prosciutto with Ginger Dressing

1 (2-lb.) honeydew melon
4 oz. thinly sliced prosciutto

Ginger Dressing:
2 pieces stem ginger preserved in syrup
2 tablespoons stem-ginger syrup
3 tablespoons vegetable oil
1 teaspoon lemon juice
Freshly ground pepper

1. Cut melon lengthwise into quarters. Discard seeds; remove peel. Cut each peeled melon quarter into 4 long slices, making a total of 16 slices.
2. Cut ham into long slices about 2 inches wide.
3. Arrange melon slices and ham slices alternatively on a serving platter.
4. To make dressing, finely chop stem ginger; place in a small bowl. Beat in ginger syrup, oil, lemon juice and pepper.
5. Pour dressing evenly over melon and ham. Cover and refrigerate 30 minutes before serving. Makes 4 starters.

Clockwise from top left: Pears with Blue Cheese, Peaches & Cream Salad, Melon & Prosciutto with Ginger Dressing

Fennel & Apple Salad

2 fennel bulbs, about 1 lb. total weight
4 small or 3 large apples
1/2 cup coarsely chopped nuts
1/2 cup Mayonnaise, page 78, or prepared mayonnaise
5 tablespoons orange juice
Salt
Freshly ground pepper

---

1. Cut fennel bulbs in half lengthwise. Trim off feathery green leaves; reserve for garnish. Slice fennel very finely. Place fennel slices in a large bowl.
2. Quarter apples; remove cores. Cut apple quarters into thin slices. Add apple slices and nuts to fennel.
3. In a small bowl, combine mayonnaise and orange juice until smooth. Season with salt and pepper.
4. Pour dressing over salad; toss to coat with dressing.
5. Garnish with reserved fennel leaves. Serve immediately with cold roast meat or cold poached fish. Makes 4 to 6 dinner salads.

Crunchy Green Salad with Blue-Cheese Dressing

1/4 head green cabbage
1/2 bunch broccoli
1 medium zucchini
1 small green bell pepper, thinly sliced
1 celery stalk, thinly sliced
1/2 cup Yogurt & Blue-Cheese Dressing, page 79, or prepared blue-cheese dressing

---

1. Slice cabbage very thinly, discarding any core. Place sliced cabbage in a large bowl.
2. Divide broccoli into flowerets; discard tough stalks. Add flowerets to cabbage.
3. Cut off and discard zucchini ends; slice trimmed zucchini as thinly as possible. Add to cabbage and broccoli.
4. Add pepper slices and celery to bowl. Pour dressing over vegetables; toss well.
5. Cover and refrigerate 1 hour before serving. Makes 4 to 6 dinner salads.

Left to right: Fennel & Apple Salad, Crunchy Green Salad with Blue-Cheese Dressing, Beef & Radish Salad

Bread & Cheese Salad

2 cups plain croutons
1/2 cup Oil & Vinegar Dressing, page 78, or
   prepared dressing
1 teaspoon chopped fresh thyme or 1/2 teaspoon
   dried leaf thyme
8 celery stalks, sliced crosswise
4 tomatoes, cut into wedges
8 oz. Cheddar cheese or other hard cheese
Lettuce leaves or endive leaves, if desired

To garnish:
Celery leaves

1. Place croutons in a large bowl.
2. In a small bowl, combine dressing and thyme; pour over bread. Toss until croutons are coated with dressing.
3. Add celery and tomatoes; toss lightly.
4. Cut cheese into small cubes or strips; add to salad.
5. Serve immediately. Or, cover and refrigerate several hours.
6. Serve from bowl. Or, arrange lettuce or endive on a serving plate; top with salad. Garnish with celery leaves. Makes 4 main-dish servings.

Beef & Radish Salad

1 lb. cold roast beef
1 bunch radishes with leaves
1/2 cup broken walnut halves

Dressing:
1/4 cup walnut oil or olive oil
2 tablespoons orange juice
1 tablespoon white-wine vinegar
Salt
Freshly ground pepper

1. Thinly slice beef; cut slices into 1-1/2" x 1/2" strips; place in a medium bowl.
2. Reserve 2 or 3 radishes and radish leaves for garnishing. For instructions on making radish roses, see illustrations below. Thinly slice remaining radishes; add sliced radishes to beef.
3. Add walnuts.
4. In a small bowl, combine dressing ingredients. Pour dressing over beef mixture. Toss to coat with dressing. Cover and refrigerate until served.
5. Spoon beef-and-radish salad into a serving bowl; garnish with radish roses and radish leaves. Makes 4 main-dish servings.

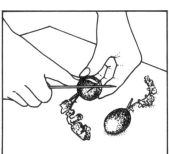

1/To make radish garnishes, cut vertically through center of radish almost to stem end. Give radish a 1/2 turn; make another cut. Repeat cuts at 1/8-inch intervals.

2/Place cut radishes in iced water until cuts open. Leave stem on, if desired.

Seviche

1-1/2 lb. white fish fillets, skin removed
1/4 cup fresh lemon juice or lime juice
4 medium tomatoes
1 small green bell pepper
1 (4-inch) cucumber piece
2 tablespoons vegetable oil
1 tablespoon finely chopped onion
1 tablespoon ketchup
Salt
Freshly ground black pepper
Few drops hot-pepper sauce, if desired

To serve:
1 small head lettuce, shredded
Lime or lemon slices

---

1. Cut fish into thin strips; place in a medium bowl.
2. Pour lemon juice or lime juice over fish; stir until fish is coated. Cover and refrigerate at least 2 hours or until fish has turned white and opaque and looks cooked.
3. Meanwhile prepare vegetables. Peel tomatoes. Remove and discard seeds; dice tomatoes.
4. Cut bell pepper into quarters; remove and discard seeds. Dice bell pepper. Cut cucumber into slices; dice slices.
5. Combine marinated fish, diced tomatoes, diced bell pepper and diced cucumber
6. In a small bowl, combine oil, onion, ketchup, salt, black pepper and hot-pepper sauce, if desired. Stir dressing into salad. Serve immediately, or cover and refrigerate up to 8 hours.
7. To serve, divide lettuce among individual plates. Spoon Seviche over lettuce; garnish each serving with a lime or lemon twist. Makes 4 main-dish servings or 6 starters.

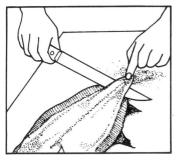 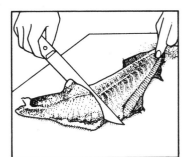

1/To skin a fish fillet, place fillet skin-side down. Starting at the tail, insert a knife between flesh and skin.

2/Carefully run knife towards the head, keeping blade slanting downwards. Sprinkle salt on the work surface to keep fish from slipping.

Inca Salad

1/4 cup Oil & Vinegar Dressing, page 78, or
  other dressing
Few drops hot-pepper sauce
2 medium, ripe avocados
2 cups diced, cooked, peeled potatoes
1 (6-1/2-oz.) can tuna, water pack, drained, flaked
Lettuce leaves, if desired

To garnish:
4 small fresh chili peppers or cucumber slices

---

1. To make a hot-chili dressing, pour oil-and-vinegar dressing into a medium bowl; blend in hot-pepper sauce to taste.
2. Cut avocados in half. Remove seeds and peel. Cut peeled avocados into small cubes. Lightly toss avocado cubes in dressing.
3. Add potato cubes and tuna to avocado mixture. Toss gently; do not mash avocado cubes.
4. Line a serving dish or individual plates with lettuce leaves, if desired; mound avocado salad on top.
5. Garnish with chili flowers. To make chili flowers, see illustrations below. Or, garnish salad with cucumber twists. Makes 4 main-dish servings or 6 starters.

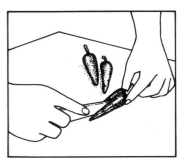 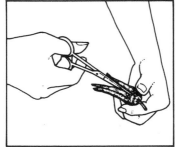

1/Make several longs cuts, starting 1/2 inch from stem end.

2/With scissors, make additional cuts for fine petals.

3/Place cut chilies in iced water until petals open.

Left to right: Seviche, Inca Salad

Russian Salad with Tongue

4 medium potatoes, peeled
2 large carrots
Salt
1 cup sliced celery, or 1 medium turnip, peeled, diced
1 (10-oz.) pkg. frozen green beans or green peas
8 to 10 thin slices cooked tongue

Dressing:
1/2 cup Mayonnaise, page 78, or prepared mayonnaise
2/3 cup dairy sour cream or plain yogurt
1 tablespoon chopped pickle
1 tablespoon capers

To garnish:
1 tablespoon capers
Pickle fans, see below

---

1. Place whole potatoes, carrots and salt in a large saucepan; cover with cold water. Bring to a boil; simmer 15 to 20 minutes or until tender but not soft. Drain; cool to room temperature.
2. In a medium saucepan, cook celery or turnip in boiling salted water about 15 minutes or until crisp-tender. Cook beans or peas 3 to 4 minutes in salted water. Drain vegetables; cool to room temperature.
3. Dice cooled potatoes and carrots; place diced vegetables in a large bowl. Stir in cooled celery or turnip and beans or peas.
4. To make dressing, in a small bowl, combine mayonnaise and sour cream or yogurt; stir in pickles and 1 tablespoon capers.
5. Pour dressing over vegetables; toss to coat with dressing.
6. Serve immediately. Or, cover and refrigerate up to 24 hours. To serve, arrange slices of tongue around edge of a platter. Pile Russian Salad in center; garnish with 1 tablespoon capers and pickle fans. Makes 4 main-dish servings.

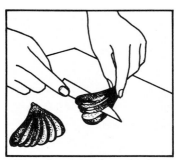

1/To make pickle fans, thinly slice pickle horizontally to within 1/2 inch of stem end. Spread slices apart to form a fan.

Maryland Chicken Salad

1 tablespoon all-purpose flour
Salt
Freshly ground pepper
1 (2-1/2- to 3-lb.) broiler-fryer chicken, cut up
1 egg, beaten
1/2 cup dry bread crumbs
1/4 cup butter or margarine
1 tablespoon vegetable oil
4 small firm bananas
1 (12-oz.) can whole-kernel corn
1 bunch watercress
1 cup Yogurt Dressing, page 79

---

1. In a plastic bag, combine flour, salt and pepper. Add chicken pieces; shake to coat. Dip floured chicken in egg; coat with bread crumbs.
2. Heat butter or margarine and oil in a large skillet. Add coated chicken; sauté over medium heat 15 to 20 minutes, turning until chicken is golden brown and tender. With tongs, place cooked chicken on paper towels to drain. Reserve oil mixture for cooking bananas.
3. Peel bananas; cut in half lengthwise. Heat reserved oil mixture; add banana halves. Sauté, turning once, until lightly browned. Drain on paper towels.
4. Drain corn; set aside.
5. Arrange warm chicken on a large platter; top with warm bananas. Surround with drained corn. Garnish with watercress. Serve dressing separately. Makes 4 to 6 main-dish servings.

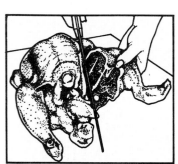

1/To cut up a chicken, cut through joints connecting thighs to body.

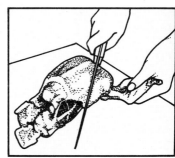

2/Cut through joints connecting wings to body.

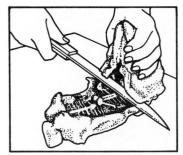

3/Remove breast by cutting along rib bones.

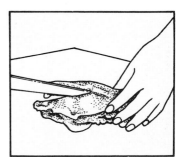

4/Cut through breast at breast bone.

Corn Salad

2 (17-oz.) cans whole-kernel corn or 2 (10-oz.) pkgs.
  frozen whole-kernel corn
Salt
1/4 cup corn oil
1 tablespoon white-wine vinegar
1 tablespoon Worcestershire sauce
1 tablespoon ketchup
1 tablespoon brown sugar
1 tablespoon grated onion
1/3 cup raisins
1 red or green bell pepper, finely chopped

1. In a medium saucepan, cook frozen corn in salted boiling water according to package directions. Drain; cool to room temperature. If using canned corn; drain. Set aside.
2. Pour corn oil into a medium bowl. Beat in vinegar, Worcestershire sauce, ketchup, sugar and onion.
3. Stir in raisins and bell pepper. Stir in drained corn until combined.
4. Serve immediately, or cover and refrigerate up to 2 days. Serve with hamburgers or barbecued meat. Makes 4 dinner salads.

Top to bottom: Corn Salad, Maryland Chicken Salad with Yogurt Dressing

Marinated Mushrooms

2 tablespoons olive oil or corn oil
2 onions, thinly sliced
1 celery stalk, thinly sliced
1 large garlic clove, crushed
2 bacon slices, chopped
1/2 cup red wine
2 medium tomatoes, peeled, quartered, seeded
1 tablespoon fresh thyme leaves or 1-1/2 teaspoons
    dried leaf thyme
1 bay leaf
Salt
Freshly ground pepper
1 (3-inch) cinnamon stick, if desired
1 lb. button mushrooms, wiped

To garnish:
1 tablespoon fresh thyme leaves, if desired

1. Heat oil in a large saucepan. Add onions, celery, garlic and bacon; sauté over medium heat 5 minutes, stirring occasionally.
2. Stir in wine, tomatoes, thyme, bay leaf, salt, pepper and cinnamon stick, if desired. Bring to a boil; reduce heat.
3. Cut large mushrooms into halves or quarters; leave small mushrooms whole. Add mushrooms to saucepan.
4. Simmer 10 minutes. Cool in liquid; remove and discard bay leaf and cinnamon stick. Refrigerate at least 1 hour or up to 24 hours.
5. Drain mushrooms, discarding marinade. Place in a serving bowl; sprinkle with fresh thyme leaves, if desired. Makes 4 dinner salads or 4 starters.

Lemon & Thyme Mushrooms

8 oz. large, flat mushrooms
1 small lemon
6 tablespoons olive oil
1 tablespoon fresh thyme leaves or 1 teaspoon
    dried leaf thyme
1 tablespoon chopped fresh parsley
Salt
Freshly ground pepper
1 small garlic clove, if desired, crushed

1. Slice mushrooms crosswise into long thin strips; arrange in a shallow serving dish.
2. Grate lemon peel into a small bowl; squeeze lemon juice into bowl.
3. Whisk in olive oil, thyme, parsley, salt, pepper and garlic, if desired.
4. Pour dressing over mushrooms. Refrigerate at least 1 hour or up to 24 hours. Makes 4 dinner salads or 4 starters.

Variation
Lemon & Thyme Mushrooms with Shrimp: Stir 8 ounces deveined, peeled, cooked shrimp in salad before serving.

Sweet & Sour Chinese Salad

2 tablespoons corn oil
1 tablespoon honey
1 tablespoon soy sauce
2 tablespoons lemon juice
4 oz. mushrooms, sliced
6 green onions, chopped
4 oz. bean sprouts (1 cup)
1/2 head Chinese cabbage, coarsely shredded

1. Combine oil, honey, soy sauce and lemon juice in a large bowl.
2. Stir mushrooms into soy-honey mixture until coated.
3. Stir in green onions and bean sprouts. Add Chinese cabbage; toss to coat with dressing. Serve with pork chops, spareribs or cold roast pork. Makes 4 dinner salads.

Top to bottom: Sweet & Sour Chinese Salad, Marinated Mushrooms

Risotto Salad

2 tablespoons vegetable oil
4 bacon slices, chopped
1 medium onion, chopped
8 oz. chicken livers, chopped
1 garlic clove, if desired, crushed
1-1/4 cups uncooked long-grain white rice
2-1/2 cups chicken stock
1/2 teaspoon dried leaf oregano or dried leaf marjoram
Salt
Freshly ground pepper
1 (7-oz.) can whole-kernel corn, drained
1/2 cup Oil & Vinegar Dressing, page 78, or
    prepared dressing

To garnish:
1 tablespoon chopped fresh parsley

This chicken-liver risotto is cooked exactly as a hot risotto. While it is still hot, oil-and-vinegar dressing is stirred into the rice mixture to add extra flavor. Cool the risotto before serving.

1. Heat oil in a large saucepan. Add bacon and onion; sauté 3 minutes.
2. Add chicken livers and garlic, if desired. Cook 2 minutes, stirring occasionally.
3. Stir in rice; cook 1 minute. Stir in chicken stock, oregano or marjoram, salt, pepper and corn. Bring to a boil; reduce heat.
4. Cover pan; simmer 15 to 20 minutes or until all stock is absorbed and rice is tender.
5. Transfer hot risotto to a bowl; stir in 1/2 of dressing. Cool to room temperature. Serve immediately, or cover and refrigerate up to 24 hours. Bring to room temperature before serving.
6. Immediately before serving, stir in remaining dressing; sprinkle with chopped parsley. Serve with a green salad. Makes 4 light main-dish servings.

Variation
Substitute long-grain brown rice for white rice. Use 3 cups of chicken stock; increase cooking time to 30 to 35 minutes. For perfect cooked rice, after all liquid has been absorbed and rice is tender, remove pan from heat. Do not remove lid; let stand a few minutes. The rice will fluff up in its own steam.

Left to right: Risotto Salad, Provençal Stuffed Eggs

Provençal Potato Salad

1 (2-oz.) can anchovy fillets
1/2 teaspoon Italian seasoning
1 teaspoon chopped fresh parsley, if desired
3-3/4 cups thinly sliced peeled potatoes (about 1-1/4 lb.)
1 small onion, thinly sliced
2 small tomatoes, thinly sliced
1 tablespoon olive oil

1. Place anchovies with their oil in a small bowl. Add Italian seasoning and parsley, if desired; mash into a paste. Set aside.
2. Preheat oven to 375F (190C). Grease a 1-1/2-quart baking dish.
3. Arrange 1/3 of potatoes in bottom of dish. Cover with 1/2 of onion and 1/2 of tomatoes; spread lightly with 1/2 of anchovy paste. Repeat with 1/3 of potatoes and remaining 1/2 of onion, tomatoes and anchovy paste. Top with remaining 1/3 of potatoes. Brush top with oil.
4. Bake in preheated oven 1 to 1-1/4 hours or until top is golden and potatoes are tender. Cool to room temperature. Serve immediately, or cover and refrigerate up to 24 hours. Bring to room temperature before serving. Makes 4 to 6 dinner salads.

Provençal Stuffed Eggs

16 pitted black olives
1 (2-oz.) can anchovy fillets
1 tablespoon capers
4 hard-cooked eggs

To serve:
Shredded lettuce
4 tomatoes, sliced
1 tablespoon chopped fresh parsley
2 tablespoons Oil & Vinegar Dressing, page 78, or
   prepared dressing

1. Place 12 olives in a medium bowl; reserve remaining olives. Add anchovies with their oil and capers to bowl; pound into a paste.
2. Cut eggs in half lengthwise. Remove yolks; mash yolks into anchovy mixture.
3. Divide egg-yolk mixture among egg-white halves. Cut reserved olives in half. Top each stuffed egg half with an olive half.
4. To serve, arrange lettuce on a platter. Arrange tomato slices in center; sprinkle tomatoes with parsley and dressing. Arrange stuffed eggs around edge of platter. Makes 4 starters.

Stuffed Peppers

1 cup uncooked long-grain white rice
2 cups water
Salt
4 red, yellow or green bell peppers
2 small tomatoes, peeled, chopped
1/2 cup chopped walnuts
1/3 cup raisins
2 tablespoons chopped fresh parsley
1/4 cup Oil & Vinegar Dressing, page 78, or
    prepared dressing
Freshly ground black pepper
1/2 cup water or chicken stock

1. In a medium saucepan, combine rice, water and salt. Cover; bring to a boil. Reduce heat; simmer about 20 minutes or until all water has been absorbed and rice is tender.
2. While rice is cooking, cut bell peppers in half lengthwise; discard core and seeds.
3. When rice is cooked, stir in chopped tomatoes, walnuts, raisins, parsley, dressing, salt and black pepper.
4. Spoon rice mixture into bell-pepper halves; place stuffed peppers in a roasting pan or ovenproof dish. Pour water or stock around peppers. Cover pan with a lid or foil.
5. Bake in preheated oven about 45 minutes or until peppers are tender. Cool to room temperature. Serve immediately, or cover and refrigerate up to 24 hours. Bring to room temperature before serving. Makes 4 main-dish servings or 8 starters.

Variations

Stuffed Eggplant: Halve 2 eggplants lengthwise; scoop out centers. Chop centers; place in a colander. Sprinkle lightly with salt. Sprinkle eggplant shells with salt; let stand upside-down 30 minutes to drain. Rinse shells and chopped centers; pat dry with paper towels. Combine rinsed chopped eggplant and rice mixture; spoon into eggplant shells. Bake in preheated oven 1 hour or until tender.

Stuffed Zucchini: Halve 4 zucchini lengthwise; scoop out centers. Combine chopped centers and rice mixture; spoon into zucchini. Bake in preheated oven 30 to 45 minutes or until tender.

Stuffed Onions: Peel 4 large onions; slice off root ends to make bottoms level. Place onions in a medium saucepan; cover with water. Bring to a boil; simmer 10 minutes. Drain; set aside to cool. Slice off tops; reserve tops for lids. Pull out centers; chop. Combine chopped onion and rice mixture; spoon into onions. Replace lids. Bake in preheated oven 45 minutes or until tender.

Tomatoes: Slice off tops of 8 small or 4 large tomatoes; reserve tops for lids. Scoop out pulp. Combine tomato pulp and rice mixture; spoon into tomatoes. Replace lids. Bake 15 to 20 minutes or until hot.

Stuffed Vegetables

Chicken Salad Véronique

1/4 cup vegetable oil
1 garlic clove, if desired
4 boneless, skinless chicken-breast halves
1/2 cup sliced almonds

Sour-Cream Dressing:
2/3 cup dairy sour cream
1 tablespoon white vermouth or dry white wine
Salt
Freshly ground pepper

To serve:
Curly endive
8 oz. seedless green grapes

This is a cold version of a classic hot French dish, Chicken Véronique. It is an excellent choice for a luncheon or buffet. It is attractive and can be prepared ahead.

1. Heat oil in a large skillet; add garlic, if desired. Add chicken; sauté 10 minutes or until golden brown, turning once.
2. Remove chicken from skillet with tongs; drain on paper towels. Discard garlic. Add almonds to skillet; sauté, stirring constantly, until lightly browned. Remove from skillet; drain on paper towels. Cool chicken and almonds to room temperature. Reserve cooking oil for dressing; set aside to cool.
3. To make dressing, in a small bowl, combine sour cream, cooled cooking oil, vermouth or white wine, salt and pepper. Dressing, almonds and chicken can be refrigerated in separate containers up to 1 day.
4. To serve, arrange endive leaves on a serving plate; place cold chicken breasts on top.
5. Pour dressing over chicken; sprinkle with browned almonds and grapes. Makes 4 main-dish servings.

Variation
To make serving easier, cut cooled chicken breasts into bite-size pieces. Fold chicken pieces, grapes and almonds into dressing. Spoon salad into a shallow serving bowl lined with lettuce leaves.

Orchard Salad

Grated peel and juice of 2 small oranges
1 tablespoon chopped fresh mint or parsley
Salt
Freshly ground pepper
3 firm, medium pears
3 small apples
1/2 cup fresh blackberries
1/2 cup coarsely chopped almonds or other nuts

1. Place orange peel and orange juice in a medium bowl. Stir in mint or parsley, salt and pepper.
2. Quarter and core pears and apples. Cut each quarter crosswise into wedge-shaped slices. Add sliced pears and apples to orange-juice mixture; toss well.
3. Gently stir in blackberries and nuts. Serve with rich meats, such as pork and duck. Makes 4 to 6 dinner salads.

Leek, Orange & Nut Salad

1 lb. leeks

Orange Dressing:
2 medium oranges
1/4 cup olive oil
Salt
Freshly ground pepper

To garnish:
1/2 cup chopped nuts

If a milder flavor is preferred, blanch sliced leeks in boiling water 1 to 2 minutes before using.

1. Cut off roots and green tops of leeks. Make a long, lengthwise cut in each leek, starting at green end. Pull open; plunge leeks, green ends first, into cold water to flush out any dirt from insides. Wash leeks carefully to remove all dirt between layers. Slice leeks into thin rounds. Separate into rings.
2. To make dressing, shred orange peel into long thin strips. Place orange-peel strips into a medium bowl. Squeeze orange juice into bowl; whisk in olive oil, salt and pepper.
3. When dressing is combined, stir in sliced leeks. Toss until leeks are coated with dressing.
4. Marinate 1 hour, or cover and refrigerate up to 8 hours to soften leeks. Serve with chicken or lamb. Sprinkle with nuts before serving. Makes 4 to 6 dinner salads.

Chicken-Liver Ring

1 (1/4-oz.) envelope plus 1 teaspoon unflavored
  gelatin powder
2-1/2 cups chicken broth
1 teaspoon Worcestershire sauce
2 tablespoons dry sherry
1 bunch green onions, trimmed, sliced
2 tablespoons butter or margarine
1/2 lb. chicken livers, trimmed, coarsely chopped

To garnish:
1 carton radish sprouts

1. In a small saucepan, combine gelatin and 1/4 cup broth.
Stir well; let stand 3 minutes. Stir over low heat until gelatin dissolves. Add remaining broth and Worcestershire
sauce; stir until blended. Remove from heat; stir in sherry.

2. Rinse a 5-cup ring mold in cold water. Pour about 3/4
cup gelatin mixture into mold; set aside to cool to room
temperature. Scatter about 1/2 of onions over gelatin
mixture. Refrigerate until almost firm.
3. Melt butter or margarine in a small skillet. Add chicken
livers; sauté 4 to 5 minutes or until livers are no longer
pink. Remove livers with a slotted spoon; drain on paper
towels. Cool completely.
4. Arrange cooled chicken livers and remaining onions
over gelled gelatin mixture. Slowly pour remaining gelatin
mixture into mold. Refrigerate until completely set.
5. To serve, run the tip of a sharp knife around edge of
mold. Invert mold on a serving plate. Wet a dish towel
with hot water; wring dry. Place hot towel around mold a
few seconds. Remove towel and mold. Garnish with
sprouts. Makes 4 to 6 main-dish servings.

Clockwise from top left: Orchard Salad; Chicken Salad
Véronique; Chicken-Liver Ring; Leek, Orange & Nut Salad

Winter

Leeks à la Grecque

1/2 cup water
1/2 cup white wine
2 tablespoons olive oil
Grated peel of 1 lemon
2 tablespoons lemon juice
1 shallot or small onion, thinly sliced
1 small celery stalk with leaves
1 parsley sprig
1/4 teaspoon dried leaf thyme
1 bay leaf
1/4 teaspoon salt
6 peppercorns
6 coriander seeds or 1/4 teaspoon ground coriander
1 lb. leeks

If desired, leeks may be sliced into 3/4-inch pieces rather than left whole. Pieces will cook more quickly and are more suitable as a side dish.

1. In a large saucepan, combine water, wine, olive oil, lemon peel, lemon juice, shallot or onion, celery, parsley, thyme, bay leaf, salt, peppercorns and coriander. Cover pan; bring to a boil. Simmer 10 minutes.
2. Cut off roots and green tops of leeks, so that each leek measures about 7 inches long.
3. Make a long, lengthwise cut in each leek, starting at green end. Pull open; plunge leeks, green ends first, into cold water to flush out any dirt from insides. Wash leeks carefully to remove all dirt between layers.
4. Place prepared leeks in simmering water. Cover and simmer 10 to 15 minutes or until leeks are tender.
5. Remove leeks from pan with a slotted spoon; place in a serving dish.
6. Boil cooking liquid until reduced to 1/2 cup. Pour reduced cooking liquid over leeks, removing herbs and spices, if desired. Let stand until cool. Serve immediately, or cover and refrigerate up to 24 hours. Makes 4 dinner salads or 4 starters.

Moussaka Salad

1 (1-1/2-lb.) eggplant
1 tablespoon salt
About 1/2 cup vegetable oil
1 large onion, chopped
1-1/2 lb. lean ground lamb or beef
1 teaspoon tomato paste
Freshly ground pepper
1 garlic clove, if desired, crushed
1 large tomato, thinly sliced
3 eggs
1 tablespoon fresh marjoram or 1-1/2 teaspoons dried leaf marjoram

1. Cut eggplant into 1/8-inch slices. Place slices in a colander; sprinkle with salt. Stand colander on a plate; let drain 30 minutes.
2. Preheat oven to 350F (175C). Rinse eggplant slices; pat dry with paper towels.
3. Heat 3 tablespoons oil in a large skillet. Add rinsed eggplant slices, a few at a time. Sauté until golden brown on both sides, adding remaining eggplant and additional oil as necessary. Remove slices with a slotted spoon. Drain on paper towels.
4. Add onion to skillet; sauté 5 minutes. Add meat; sauté 5 to 10 minutes, stirring until lightly browned. Stir in tomato paste, salt, pepper and garlic, if desired.
5. Lightly grease a 1-quart casserole or 4 individual 1-cup casseroles. Arrange eggplant slices, overlapping, over bottom and side of dish or dishes, reserving enough to cover top or tops. Arrange tomato slices over eggplant slices on bottom.
6. Spoon meat mixture into eggplant-lined casserole. Beat eggs with marjoram, pepper and salt. Pour eggs over meat mixture; cover with remaining eggplant slices.
7. Bake in preheated oven 30 minutes for 1 large dish and 15 to 20 minutes for smaller dishes or until top is golden and egg mixture is set. Cool to room temperature. Serve immediately, or cover and refrigerate up to 24 hours.
8. Run a knife around edge to loosen moussaka; invert on a serving plate or individual salad plates. Remove mold or molds. Surround with endive leaves. Cut large moussaka into wedges to serve. Makes 4 dinner salads or 4 starters.

Top to bottom: Moussaka Salad, Leeks à la Grecque

Red-Bean & Broccoli Salad

1 (15-oz.) can red kidney beans
8 oz. broccoli
1/2 cup Oil & Vinegar Dressing, page 78, or
    prepared dressing
2 celery stalks, thinly sliced
2 green onions, thinly sliced

1. Drain kidney beans; rinse with cold water.
2. Divide broccoli into flowerets; set aside.
3. Place rinsed beans in a medium bowl; stir in dressing. Add broccoli flowerets, celery and green onions; toss to coat with dressing.
4. Cover and refrigerate 3 to 4 hours to allow flavors to blend. Makes 4 dinner salads.

Broccoli Niçoise

1 lb. broccoli
1 (6-1/2-oz.) can tuna, oil pack, drained, flaked
2 hard-cooked eggs
1 (2-oz.) can anchovy fillets, drained
8 small pitted black olives
1/2 cup Oil & Vinegar Dressing, page 78, or
    prepared dressing

1. Cut broccoli into small flowerets; cook in a little boiling, salted water 5 to 8 minutes or until crisp-tender. Drain; rinse with cold water to cool quickly.
2. When broccoli is cold, place on bottom of a shallow serving dish or platter. Arrange tuna on broccoli.
3. Cut hard-cooked eggs into wedges; place egg wedges, anchovies and olives on tuna. Salad can be covered and refrigerated 6 to 8 hours at this point.
4. To complete salad, pour dressing over salad. For a main-dish salad, serve with French bread. Makes 4 light main-dish servings or 6 starters.

Red-Bean & Broccoli Salad

Pickled-Herring Salad

Pickled-Herring Salad

4 fresh herring, ready to cook
Salt
Freshly ground pepper
1 medium carrot, thinly sliced
1 medium onion, thinly sliced
1 apple, if desired, peeled, sliced
6 peppercorns
2 bay leaves
1/2 cup white-wine vinegar
1/2 cup water

1. Preheat oven to 350F (175C). Remove backbones from herring without removing tails. Press down on boned herring to flatten.
2. Sprinkle herring with salt and pepper; roll each herring, beginning at head end. Place rolled herrings in a shallow ovenproof dish, tails pointing upward.
3. Scatter carrot, onion and apple, if desired, over herring. Add peppercorns, bay leaves, vinegar and water. Cover with a lid or foil.
4. Bake in preheated oven about 20 minutes or until fish tests done. Cool to room temperature. Serve immediately, or cover and refrigerate up to 24 hours. Makes 4 starters.

Sunchoke Salad

1-1/2 lb. sunchokes (Jerusalem artichokes)
Salt

Dressing:
Grated peel and juice of 1/2 lemon
1/4 cup olive oil
1 tablespoon fresh thyme leaves
1 tablespoon chopped fresh parsley
Freshly ground pepper

1. Place sunchokes and salt in a medium saucepan; cover with cold water. Cover pan; bring to a boil. Simmer about 15 minutes or until sunchokes are crisp-tender. Drain; cool. Peel cooled sunchokes.
2. To make dressing, in a small bowl, combine lemon peel, lemon juice, olive oil, thyme, parsley, salt and pepper.
3. Slice peeled sunchokes; place slices in a serving bowl. Pour dressing over sunchoke slices; stir to coat with dressing. Cover and refrigerate until chilled, or refrigerate up to 24 hours. Makes 4 dinner salads.

Winter Root Salad

6 tablespoons orange juice
2 tablespoons white-wine vinegar
3 tablespoons vegetable oil
Salt
Freshly ground pepper
1/3 cup raisins
1 small celeriac, peeled
3 carrots, peeled

Toss celeriac in dressing immediately after cutting to prevent browning.

1. In a medium bowl, combine orange juice, vinegar and oil. Stir in salt, pepper and raisins.
2. Cut celeriac and carrots into julienne strips; add strips to orange dressing. Stir until coated with dressing.
3. Cover and refrigerate at least 1 hour or up to 24 hours before serving, stirring occasionally. Makes 4 dinner salads.

Turnip & Watercress Salad

4 to 5 turnips
2 tablespoons lemon juice
Salt
Freshly ground pepper
1 large bunch watercress, coarse stalks removed
1 tablespoon Dijon-style mustard
1/2 cup Mayonnaise, page 78, or prepared mayonnaise

---

1. Peel turnips; coarsely shred into long thin strips with a shredder. Or, cut into julienne strips with a knife.
2. Place turnip strips in a medium bowl. Add lemon juice, salt and pepper. Toss until blended. Let stand about 30 minutes to soften turnips.
3. Coarsely chop watercress; add to turnips.
4. In a small bowl, blend mustard and mayonnaise. Add to salad; toss to coat turnip strips and watercress with dressing. Serve immediately. Makes 4 dinner salads.

Left to right: Winter Root Salad, Turnip & Watercress Salad,
Winter Leaf Salad, Christmas Coleslaw

Winter Leaf Salad

1/2 head curly endive
1 large head Belgian endive
1 head radicchio
1 bunch watercress
Leaves from celery heart
1/4 cup Oil & Vinegar Dressing, page 78, or
   prepared dressing

---

1. Separate curly endive into individual leaves; tear into bite-size pieces. Place endive pieces in a salad bowl.
2. Slice Belgian endive crosswise into thin rings; add to salad bowl.
3. Separate radicchio; tear into bite-size pieces. Add radicchio pieces to salad bowl.
4. Cut off coarse watercress stalks; separate celery leaves. Add watercress and celery leaves to salad. Serve immediately, or cover and refrigerate up to 6 to 8 hours.
5. Immediately before serving, pour dressing over salad; toss until all leaves are coated with dressing. Makes 4 dinner salads.

Christmas Coleslaw

1/4 head red cabbage
1/4 head white cabbage
2 red-skinned apples
1/2 cup chopped nuts
1/2 cup Mayonnaise, page 78, or prepared mayonnaise
2 tablespoons Oil & Vinegar Dressing, page 78, or
   prepared dressing

To garnish:
1 tablespoon chopped fresh parsley

---

1. Thinly shred both cabbages, discarding cores; place in a large bowl.
2. Cut apples into quarters; remove cores. Cut quarters into very thin slices; add to cabbage.
3. Add chopped nuts.
4. In a small bowl, combine mayonnaise and oil-and-vinegar dressing. Pour over cabbage salad; toss until salad is coated with dressing. Serve immediately, or cover and refrigerate 3 to 4 hours.
5. To serve, place salad in a serving bowl; sprinkle with parsley. Makes 4 to 6 dinner salads.

Spinach-Noodle Salad

8 oz. spinach noodles
Salt
1/2 cup Oil & Vinegar Dressing, page 78, or
  prepared dressing
4 oz. mushrooms, thinly sliced
1 small garlic clove, if desired, crushed
4 oz. cooked ham, thinly sliced
1/3 cup grated Parmesan cheese (1 oz.)

---

1. Cook noodles in a large pan of boiling salted water according to package directions until tender. Do not overcook. Drain cooked noodles.
2. In a large bowl, combine dressing, mushrooms and garlic, if desired.
3. Add warm noodles; toss until coated with dressing.
4. Cut ham into strips the same width as noodles; add to salad. Toss to combine. Serve immediately, or cover and refrigerate up to 24 hours. Bring to room temperature before serving.
5. To serve, spoon into a serving bowl; sprinkle with Parmesan cheese. Makes 4 light main-dish servings or 6 to 8 starters.

Variations

For larger main-dish servings, double the amount of ham. Or, substitute 1/2 cup Yogurt Dressing, page 79, and 2 tablespoons chopped fresh parsley for oil-and-vinegar dressing.

Crab-&-Apple-Stuffed Avocados

1/4 cup Mayonnaise, page 78, or prepared mayonnaise
2 tablespoons ketchup
2 tablespoons lemon juice
Salt
Freshly ground pepper
1 apple
6 oz. cooked crabmeat, flaked
2 large ripe avocados

To garnish:
1 small head lettuce

---

1. In a medium bowl, combine mayonnaise, ketchup and lemon juice. Season with salt and pepper.
2. Cut apple into quarters; remove cores. Coarsely grate unpeeled apple into mayonnaise mixture. Stir to combine.
3. Stir in crabmeat.
4. Cut avocados in half; remove seeds. Divide filling among avocado halves. Serve immediately.
5. To serve, place lettuce leaves on a serving platter or 4 individual plates; place filled avocado halves on lettuce leaves. Makes 4 main-dish servings.

Brussels Salad

8 oz. chestnuts
12 oz. Brussels sprouts
1/2 cup Oil & Vinegar Dressing, page 78, or
  prepared dressing

---

1. Preheat oven to 450F (230C). Slit chestnut shells with a sharp knife; place chestnuts on a baking sheet.
2. Bake on top rack in preheated oven about 15 minutes or until slits have opened.
3. While chestnuts are still warm, remove shells and inner skins. Coarsely chop shelled chestnuts.
4. Trim stalk and outer leaves from Brussels sprouts. Cut trimmed Brussels sprouts in half lengthwise. Place cut-side down on a board; shred very thinly.
5. Place shredded Brussels sprouts in a serving bowl; add chopped chestnuts. Pour dressing over salad; toss to coat with dressing. Serve immediately, or cover and refrigerate 4 to 6 hours. Serve with cold roast turkey or chicken. Makes 4 dinner salads.

Top to bottom: Spinach-Noodle Salad, Crab-&-Apple-Stuffed Avocados

Tangerine-Flower Salad

4 large tangerines
1/2 cup chopped nuts
8 oz. cottage cheese (1 cup)
1/3 cup golden raisins
Salt
Freshly ground pepper

To serve:
1 small head lettuce

1. With a sharp pointed knife, cutting only through peel, make 4 shallow cuts beginning at blossom end of each tangerine. Cut almost to stem end. Pull back skin in 4 sections, leaving fruit intact. Peel skin back to make a case resembling petals of a flower, keeping skin joined at stem end; see illustration below.
2. Remove fruit; separate fruit into sections, removing white pith. Chop sections into small pieces; place in a medium bowl.
3. Stir in nuts, cottage cheese, raisins, salt and pepper.
4. Spoon filling into tangerine shells. Arrange lettuce leaves on 4 individual plates. Place filled tangerine shells on lettuce leaves. Serve immediately. Makes 4 dinner salads.

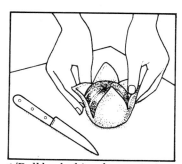
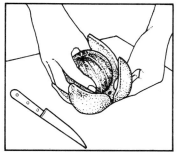

1/Pull back skin, along cuts, to make 4 sections.

2/Remove fruit.

Waldorf Salad

3 to 4 red-skinned apples
1 tablespoon lemon juice
4 celery stalks, thinly sliced crosswise
1/2 cup coarsely chopped walnuts
1/2 cup chopped dates, if desired
1/2 cup Mayonnaise, page 78, prepared mayonnaise, or Yogurt Dressing, page 79
Salt
Freshly ground pepper

To garnish:
Celery leaves
Apple slices, if desired, tossed in 1 tablespoon lemon juice

1. Quarter apples; remove cores. Chop apple quarters; place in a medium bowl. Add lemon juice; toss to prevent apples from browning.
2. Stir in celery, walnuts and dates, if desired.
3. Stir in mayonnaise or Yogurt Dressing. Season with salt and pepper.
4. Place salad in a serving dish. Garnish with celery leaves and apple slices, if desired. This salad is good with cold meats. Makes 4 dinner salads.

Variation
For a main dish, serve salad with 4 cold roast-pork slices. Or, cube about 8 ounces cold roast pork; stir pork cubes into salad, adding additional dressing, if necessary.

Pineapple & Cheese Boats

1 medium pineapple, about 2 lb.
8 oz. Cheddar cheese, cubed
1/2 cucumber, cut into cubes
1/2 cup sliced Brazil nuts
1/4 cup Oil & Vinegar Dressing, page 78, or prepared dressing
1 small head lettuce, shredded

To garnish:
1/3 cup shredded coconut, lightly toasted

1. Cut pineapple lengthwise into quarters, keeping top attached to each quarter. Cut pineapple away from peel; cut pineapple into cubes. Reserve shells.
2. In a large bowl, combine pineapple cubes, cheese, cucumber and nuts. Pour dressing over salad; toss until coated with dressing.
3. Arrange pineapple shells on a platter or individual plates. Place some lettuce on top of each pineapple shell; pile pineapple salad on lettuce.
4. Sprinkle with toasted coconut. Makes 4 light main-dish servings.

Cauliflower Polonaise Salad

1 medium cauliflower
Salt
6 tablespoons Oil & Vinegar Dressing, page 78, or
    prepared dressing
2 hard-cooked eggs, finely chopped
2 tablespoons chopped fresh parsley
Freshly ground pepper

Topping:
1/4 cup butter or margarine
1 cup fresh bread crumbs
1 small garlic clove, if desired, crushed

1. Pour water 2 inches deep in a medium saucepan; bring to a boil. Divide cauliflower into flowerets; add cauliflowerets and salt to boiling water. Boil 2 minutes. Drain; let cool to room temperature.
2. Pour dressing into a medium bowl. Stir in hard-cooked eggs, parsley, salt and pepper. Add cooked cauliflowerets; toss until coated with dressing.
3. To make topping, melt butter or margarine in a large skillet; add bread crumbs and garlic, if desired. Sauté until golden brown, stirring frequently.
4. Cauliflower salad and topping can be prepared several hours ahead; refrigerate until served. To serve, place cauliflower salad in a shallow serving dish; sprinkle with topping. Makes 4 to 6 dinner salads.

Clockwise from top left: Cauliflower Polonaise Salad, Waldorf Salad, Pineapple & Cheese Boats, Tangerine-Flower Salad

Pilaf & Curried-Chicken Salad

1 tablespoon vegetable oil
1 medium onion, chopped
1-1/4 cups uncooked long-grain white rice
2-1/2 cups water or chicken stock
1/3 cup raisins
1/3 cup chopped dried apricots
1/2 cup chopped walnuts
1 (3-inch) cinnamon stick or pinch of ground cinnamon
1 bay leaf
Salt
Freshly ground pepper
1/2 cup Oil & Vinegar Dressing, page 78, or
  prepared dressing
1-1/2 cups chopped cooked chicken
1/2 cup Curry Dressing, page 79

To garnish:
Paprika

---

1. To make pilaf, heat oil in a large saucepan. Add onion; sauté 5 minutes.
2. Add rice; cook 1 minute, stirring. Pour in water or stock; stir in raisins, apricots, walnuts, cinnamon, bay leaf, salt and pepper. Bring to a boil. Cover and simmer about 20 minutes or until rice is cooked and all water has been absorbed. Remove cinnamon stick and bay leaf.
3. Stir in dressing; while pilaf mixture is still hot, press into a 1-quart ring mold. Refrigerate until chilled or up to 24 hours.
4. In a medium bowl, combine chicken and Curry Dressing. Cover and refrigerate until chilled or up to 24 hours.
5. To serve, turn pilaf ring out on a large serving plate; remove mold. Fill center of ring with curried chicken. Sprinkle with paprika. Makes 4 main-dish servings.

Pilaf & Curried-Chicken Salad

Gado Gado

1/4 head cabbage, shredded
1 cup cut fresh green beans
2 carrots, sliced
1/2 cauliflower, divided into flowerets
Salt
4 oz. bean sprouts (1 cup)
Peanut Sauce:
1/4 cup crunchy peanut butter
Juice of 1 lemon
1/4 cup water
Few drops of hot-pepper sauce
Freshly ground pepper

To garnish:
1/2 cup salted peanuts

This is an Indonesian salad. It is normally served alone as a cold dish, but it can be served with a spicy chicken or fish curry. The peanut sauce should be thick and crunchy.

1. Cook cabbage, beans, carrots and cauliflower separately in boiling salted water a few minutes or until crisp-tender. Rinse with cold water to cool quickly. Do not cook bean sprouts.
2. To make sauce, place peanut butter in a medium bowl. Gradually blend in lemon juice and water. Stir in hot-pepper sauce to taste; season with salt and pepper.
3. In a medium bowl, combine cooked vegetables and bean sprouts; arrange in a shallow serving dish. Vegetables can be prepared 2 to 3 hours ahead; cover and refrigerate. Sauce can be prepared 24 hours ahead; cover and refrigerate. Bring to room temperature before serving.
4. Pour peanut sauce over center of salad. Garnish with peanuts. Makes 4 to 6 dinner salads.

Variation
For an authentic Indonesian flavor, substitute coconut milk for water in sauce. To make coconut milk, pour 1 cup boiling water over 1 cup shredded coconut in a medium bowl. Let stand 20 minutes. Pour through a sieve, pressing on coconut to extract all liquid. Extra coconut milk can be frozen in ice-cube trays for another use.

Mussel Salad

4 to 5 dozen fresh mussels
2 tablespoons vegetable oil
2 shallots or 1 small onion, thinly sliced or chopped
1/2 cup dry white wine
Salt
Freshly ground pepper

To serve:
1 head lettuce, shredded
2 tablespoons olive oil
1 tablespoon lemon juice
2 tablespoons chopped fresh parsley

1. Discard any mussels that have broken shells or that do not close when tapped. Wash remaining mussels under cold running water.
2. Scrub each mussel; pull away beard and scrape off any barnacles with a sharp knife. Continue washing in running water until all mussels are thoroughly cleaned and water runs clear. Drain.
3. Heat oil in a large saucepan. Add shallots or onion; sauté 5 minutes or until lightly browned.
4. Pour in wine; add salt, pepper and mussels. Cover pan; bring to a boil. Cook 5 minutes, shaking pan occasionally, or until mussels open. Discard any that do not open.
5. Remove mussels, reserving liquid. Remove cooked mussels from shells. Boil cooking liquid until reduced to 1/4 cup; cool liquid.
6. Arrange shredded lettuce in a serving dish or individual dishes. Arrange cooled mussels on lettuce.
7. Stir olive oil, lemon juice and parsley into cooled cooking liquid; pour over mussels. Serve immediately. Makes 4 main-dish servings or 6 starters.

Variation
If fresh mussels are not available, substitute 2 (8-3/4-ounce) jar mussels, drained, for fresh mussels. In a medium bowl, toss with 1/2 cup Oil & Vinegar Dressing with lemon peel, page 78, or prepared dressing; sprinkle with chopped parsley.

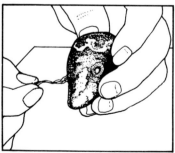

1/Pull away beards.

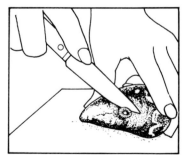

2/Scrape off any barnacles with a sharp knife.

Guacamole Salad

4 tomatoes, peeled
2 tablespoons lemon juice
1 tablespoon grated onion
1 teaspoon chopped fresh coriander or 1/2 teaspoon
  ground coriander
1/4 teaspoon hot-pepper sauce
2 ripe avocados

To garnish:
1 small head lettuce
Cilantro sprigs
Corn chips

1. Dice tomatoes; place in a medium bowl.
2. Stir in lemon juice, onion, coriander and hot-pepper sauce.
3. Cut avocados in half; pit and peel avocados. Dice peeled avocados. Add to tomato mixture. Beat with a wooden spoon until partially blended but pieces of avocado and tomato still remain.
4. Arrange lettuce leaves on 4 individual plates. Spoon guacamole salad on lettuce; garnish with coriander sprigs. Serve immediately with corn chips. Makes 4 starters.

Clockwise from top left: Guacamole Salad, Gado Gado, Mussel Salad

Vitello Tonnato

1 (2-lb.) boneless veal shoulder roast
1 onion, sliced
1 carrot, sliced
1 celery stalk, sliced
1 bay leaf
1 parsley sprig
Salt
Freshly ground pepper
2 tablespoons dry white wine or sherry

Tuna Mayonnaise:
2/3 cup Mayonnaise, page 78, or prepared mayonnaise
1/2 (6-1/2-oz.) can tuna, oil pack, undrained
1 tablespoon anchovy paste
1 teaspoon tomato paste
1 teaspoon lemon juice
Salt
Freshly ground pepper

To garnish:
1 (2-oz.) can anchovy fillets, drained
1 tablespoon capers
3 lemon slices, cut in half
Parsley sprigs

This is a popular Italian dish.

1. Place veal in a large saucepan. Add onion, carrot, celery, bay leaf, parsley, salt and pepper. Add enough cold water to almost cover veal; add wine or sherry.
2. Cover pan; bring to a boil. Reduce heat; simmer about 1-1/2 to 2 hours or until tender. Let cool in cooking liquid.
3. To make Tuna Mayonnaise, combine all ingredients in a blender or food processor fitted with a steel blade. Process until smooth. If mayonnaise is too thick, add some of cooled cooking liquid.
4. Thinly slice cooled veal. Spread each slice with 1 teaspoon of Tuna Mayonnaise; arrange slices, overlapping, on a serving platter. Cover with remaining mayonnaise.
5. Refrigerate several hours or overnight to firm mayonnaise.
6. To serve, garnish with anchovies, capers, lemon slices and parsley sprigs, as shown. This salad is ideal for a buffet lunch or dinner. Makes 4 to 6 main-dish servings.

Turkey & Cranberry Salad

1 lb. cooked turkey, cut into 1/2-inch cubes
4 large celery stalks, thinly sliced crosswise
1 green bell pepper, diced
1/2 cup chopped walnuts
2/3 cup dairy sour cream
1/4 cup whole-berry cranberry sauce
1 tablespoon red-wine vinegar
Salt
Freshly ground black pepper

To garnish:
1 bunch watercress
8 to 10 walnut halves

---

1. Place turkey cubes in a medium bowl.
2. Stir in celery, bell pepper and walnuts.
3. In a small bowl, combine sour cream, cranberry sauce, vinegar, salt and pepper.
4. Pour cranberry mixture over turkey salad; toss until combined.
5. Spoon into a serving dish; garnish with watercress and walnut halves. Makes 4 main-dish servings.

Ham & Pineapple Cornets

---

8 oz. cottage cheese (1 cup)
1 (8-oz.) can pineapple chunks, juice pack
1 small red bell pepper, finely chopped
1 celery stalk, chopped
Salt
Freshly ground black pepper
4 large or 8 small cooked-ham slices
Romaine lettuce leaves

---

1. To make filling, place cottage cheese in a medium bowl.
2. Drain pineapple; add to cottage cheese. Stir in bell pepper and celery. Season with salt and black pepper.
3. Divide filling among ham slices. Roll each slice into a cone shape; place each cone on a lettuce leaf, seam-side down. Arrange on a serving plate. Makes 4 light main-dish servings.

Top to bottom: Vitello Tonnato, Ham & Pineapple Cornets

Salad Dressings

Thousand Island Dressing

2/3 cup Mayonnaise, opposite, prepared
　　mayonnaise, or dairy sour cream
2 tablespoons milk
1 tablespoon tomato paste
1 tablespoon finely chopped red bell pepper
1 tablespoon finely chopped green bell pepper
1 tablespoon finely chopped sweet pickle
1 hard-cooked egg, if desired, finely chopped

1. Spoon mayonnaise or sour cream into a small bowl. Slowly beat in milk.
2. Stir in tomato paste until blended; stir in remaining ingredients. Cover and refrigerate until served. Serve with fish or vegetable salads. Makes about 1 cup.

Oil & Vinegar Dressing

2 tablespoons wine vinegar or lemon juice
6 tablespoons oil (olive, soybean, walnut or peanut)
Pinch of dry mustard, if desired
Pinch of salt
Freshly ground black pepper

A mixture of oils may be used, such as soybean oil blended with a more exotic one, such as walnut oil. This recipe makes enough dressing for 2 large salads.

1. Combine all ingredients in a screw top jar; shake vigorously until blended. Shake again before using. Or, combine ingredients in a small bowl; beat with a whisk until blended.
2. Store in refrigerator up to 1 week. Makes about 2/3 cup.

Variation
Add 1 or more of the following: 1 to 2 tablespoons chopped fresh herbs; grated peel of 1/2 lemon or orange; 1 small peeled garlic clove, whole for a subtle flavor or crushed for a stronger flavor; 1/4 to 1/2 teaspoon prepared brown mustard.

Mayonnaise

1 whole egg or 2 egg yolks
1/4 teaspoon dry mustard
1/4 teaspoon salt
1 tablespoon wine vinegar or lemon juice
1-1/4 cups olive oil, other vegetable oil,
　　or a combination
1 tablespoon hot water

Mayonnaise will keep, covered, in the refrigerator 2 days.

Using a blender:
1. In a blender, combine egg or egg yolks, mustard, salt and vinegar or lemon juice. Process at lowest speed until blended.
2. With blender running at lowest speed, very slowly pour in about 1/2 of oil. Mixture will begin to thicken. Add remaining oil in a slow steady stream.
3. With blender running, add water. Taste mayonnaise; add a little more vinegar or lemon juice, if necessary. Makes about 2 cups.

By hand:
1. Place a medium bowl on a folded damp cloth to keep it steady while beating.
2. In bowl, combine egg or egg yolks, mustard, salt and 2 teaspoons vinegar or lemon juice. Using a wooden spoon, small whisk or hand-held electric mixer, beat well.
3. Continue beating; beat in oil 1 drop at a time until 1/2 of oil has been added. Mixture will begin to thicken.
4. Add remaining vinegar. Beating or whisking constantly, add remaining oil in a thin, steady stream until mayonnaise is very thick. Add water; beat until blended. If mayonnaise becomes too thick to add all of oil, whisk in additional hot water; then whisk in remaining oil. Makes about 2 cups.

Variations
Green Mayonnaise: In a blender, combine 1-3/4 to 2 cups mayonnaise and about 1 cup chopped, packed watercress, sorrel or spinach, coarse stalks removed. Blend until smooth.
Anchovy Mayonnaise: In a blender, combine 1-3/4 to 2 cups mayonnaise, 1 (2-ounce) can anchovy fillets with oil and 1 tablespoon tomato paste. Blend until smooth.
Garlic Mayonnaise: In a blender, combine 1-3/4 to 2 cups mayonnaise and 1 or 2 crushed garlic cloves. Blend until smooth.

Curry Dressing

1 tablespoon vegetable oil
1 small onion, chopped
1 tablespoon curry powder
2/3 cup chicken stock
1 tablespoon apricot jam
1 teaspoon lemon juice
2/3 cup Mayonnaise, opposite, or prepared mayonnaise
2/3 cup plain yogurt or dairy sour cream
Salt
Freshly ground pepper

1. Heat oil in a medium saucepan. Add onion; sauté over low heat 5 minutes or until softened. Do not brown.
2. Stir in curry powder; cook 2 minutes, stirring constantly.
3. Gradually stir in stock; bring to a boil. Stir in jam and lemon juice; bring to a simmer. Stirring constantly, simmer 5 minutes; set aside to cool.
4. Stir mayonnaise and yogurt or sour cream into cooled curry sauce. Season with salt and pepper. Serve with root vegetables or cold chicken salad. Makes about 2 cups.

Yogurt Dressing

2/3 cup plain yogurt or dairy sour cream
1 tablespoon white-wine vinegar or lemon juice
Salt
Freshly ground pepper

1. In a small bowl, stir yogurt or sour cream until smooth.
2. Stir in vinegar or lemon juice. Season with salt and pepper; stir until blended.
3. Or, combine all ingredients in a blender or food processor fitted with a steel blade. Process until blended. Use immediately, or cover and refrigerate up to 1 week. Makes about 2/3 cup.

Variations
Herb-Yogurt Dressing: Stir in 2 tablespoons chopped fresh watercress, parsley, chives, thyme, basil or tarragon.
Yogurt & Blue-Cheese Dressing: Stir in 2 tablespoons crumbled blue cheese.
Cucumber & Mint Dressing: Coarsely grate a 1-1/2-inch piece of unpeeled cucumber. Stir grated cucumber and 1/2 teaspoon dried mint or 1 teaspoon chopped fresh mint into dressing.

Top to bottom: Mayonnaise, Oil & Vinegar Dressing, Thousand Island Dressing, Curry Dressing, Yogurt Dressing

Index